HUNTINGTON'S
PAST
REVISITED

HUNTINGTON'S
PAST
REVISITED

Written and photographed by
KERRIANN FLANAGAN BROSKY

Maple Hill Press

Back cover photograph: Diversified Photo Services

Pr͏   ͏ the United States of America

¹7-6

TABLE OF CONTENTS

DEDICATION

This book is dedicated to my husband Karl, for his constant support, understanding, faith and love, and for sticking by me when I needed it most. I couldn't have done it without you.

To my parents, Deanna and Michael, and my brother Sean and sister Kelly, for being there at all times and for giving me the encouragement and strength to go forward.

To J.F. and P.F., for giving me a second chance. Thanks for believing.

To the people of Huntington, for whom this book is written.

ACKNOWLEDGEMENTS

I would like to thank the following people and organizations who have played a role in the production and development of this book, through their assistance in research, interviews, contacts, photographs, time and support. Without all of you, this book would not have been possible.

A. Michael Flanagan, Editor; Anne Peace, Yankee Peddler; Carol Bruhns, President, Alliance for the Preservation of Coindre Hall; Cherrian and Bill Levin, Colyer House; Cold Spring Harbor Whaling Museum; Dick Simpson; Diversified Photo Services; Dorothy Koopman, Town Historian's Office; Dr. Alfred V. Sforza; Dr. Lisa Conway, Arthur Dove House; Edmund Weinman, Mother Chick's; Edward A.T. Carr; Fabrikant Chiropractic; Gary Melius, Oheka Castle, and Scott Bellando, Caretaker, Oheka Castle; Gloria Smith, East Point; Grace Taylor; Henrietta Van Siclen; Henry and Elizabeth Shea; Ilene Pedone; Janet Hanania, Huntington Regional Office of the American Red Cross; Jenny Studenroth; John Molenhoff, Jr.; Kay Carroll, Walt Whitman Birthplace; Laura Dunne, Little Cottage; Lenore and David W. Belding, Francis Robbins Estate; Louise Dougher, Greenlawn-Centerport Historical Association; Lucien Hill; Margaret and Dave Weber, Seymour House; Mitzi Caputo, Irene and Arthur Sniffin, Philip Behr, Kay White, Huntington Historical Society; Nancy Cordes, Parish Administrator, St. John's Church; Barbara Wells Fitzgerald, Director, and Mary Englemann, Curator, Northport Historical Society; Quentin Sammis and Vera Sammis Murphy; Salvatore G. Rumore, CPA; Sue Meringolo; Torkel A. Knutson; Town Archives; Tracey McCauley; Vanderbilt Museum; Vivian and Andrew Mathews, Captain Samuel Mitchell House; and Willets Shotwell.

PREFACE

Huntington has so much to offer. In recent years, it has been voted the number one place to live on Long Island, and it has been called the "most cultured town between New York City and the Hamptons." What makes it such a special place to live? I believe a lot of it has to do with the Town's history.

In our fast-paced world, more and more people are seeking to return to a way of life that existed in America years ago. Older, historic homes are now in demand. Instead of buying a new house, people are fixing up their old ones. One can still walk to town, march in a parade, and spend time with neighbors on a front porch graced with wicker furniture and the American flag. No matter where in Huntington a person may live, the feeling seems to be universal: people want to slow down and get back to the basics.

Maybe this is one of the reasons why so many people, young and old, have taken an interest in Huntington's history and in knowing what life was like here years ago. History is the key to understanding the past, and it is the door which opens to our future.

By writing about and photographing historical places and structures in the Town of Huntington, I hope to elicit greater public awareness and appreciation for our Town's history, while preserving it for generations to come. As President Abraham Lincoln once said, "I like to see a man proud of the place in which he lives."

KFB

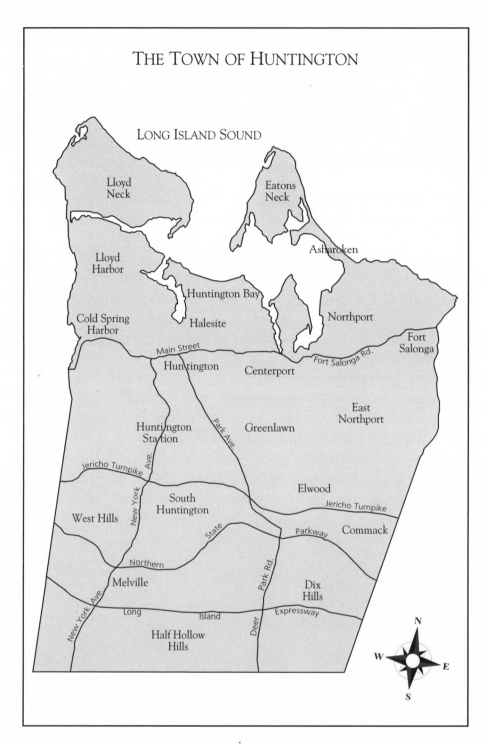

THE TOWN OF HUNTINGTON

LONG ISLAND SOUND

Lloyd
Neck

Eatons
Neck

Asharoken

Lloyd
Harbor

Huntington Bay

Northport

Cold Spring
Harbor

Halesite

Fort
Salonga

Main Street

Fort Salonga Rd.

Huntington

Centerport

East
Northport

Huntington
Station

Park Ave.

Greenlawn

Jericho Turnpike

New York Ave.

Elwood

Jericho Turnpike

West Hills

South
Huntington

State

Parkway

Commack

Northern

Park Rd.

Dix
Hills

Melville

New York Ave.

Long

Island

Deer

Expressway

Half Hollow
Hills

N

W   E

S

COLD SPRING HARBOR

THE OTTO H. KAHN ESTATE:
OHEKA CASTLE

Castles have always been romanticized in fairy tales and in real life. The enormous structures, many of which are still found in Europe, speak of wealth, beauty and enchantment. It is the stuff that dreams are made on, as they say, but for some the dream became a reality.

Otto Hermann Kahn was born in Mannheim, Germany on February 21, 1867. He was the fourth of eight children born to the well-to-do Bernhard and Emma Eberstadt Kahn. Bernhard Kahn was a very successful banker with a strong sense of family unity. He raised his children in a refined, cultural atmosphere that greatly focused on the arts. All received private tutoring at home in literature, poetry, classical and opera music, painting, sculpture and philosophy, as well as math, science, history and economics.

The young Otto Kahn was quite precocious, and by age eight he played the piano, violin and cello. In his teenage years Otto took up the hobby of writing, and by the age of sixteen, his father introduced him to the field of banking. Despite Bernhard's own position in the banking world, he taught Otto that "One must learn to obey before being fit to command," and set him up as an apprentice at a banking firm. He worked during the day, and attended school at night at a local university.

By the age of nineteen, Otto's banking career was put on hold when he entered the military, serving as a cavalryman for twelve months. When he finished his term he decided to travel instead of returning to his job, and spent several years in England, where his mother's sisters lived. Otto loved the English lifestyle, and decided to remain in London, where he obtained a position with the London branch of the Deutsche Bank. His attachment to English life grew so strong that he renounced his German citizenship and became a naturalized British subject.

Kahn never had any plans to leave London until an American banking firm, Speyer and Company of New York, offered him a position in their office. Intrigued with the idea of living in the States, Otto Kahn accepted the position and sailed to America in the summer of 1893 at the age of twenty-six.

Within three years, Kahn had made a name for himself on Wall Street, in investment banking. He married Addie Wolff on January 8, 1896. Addie was the daughter of Abraham Wolff, a partner in the banking firm of Kuhn, Loeb and Company. Abraham, seeing how successful Otto was in the banking field, made him an offer to join his company as junior partner, which Kahn accepted. In that same year, Otto had enough money to take a year off from business and tour Europe with Addie, knowing that his new job was secured.

Addie and Otto both loved the outdoors, the theater and the arts, and they resided both in Manhattan, at 8 East Sixty-Eighth Street, and in the country. Their country home, known as "Cedar Court," was built in the suburbs of Morristown, New Jersey by the architectural firm of Carrere and Hastings. The Kahns decorated their Morristown home with an extensive collection of art works they purchased while traveling in Europe. In February of 1905, a fire broke out in one of the wings of the magnificent estate, destroying over three quarters of a million dollars of personal property. After the incident and from that day forward, Otto Kahn developed an excessive fear of fire. The destroyed area of the Italian-style villa was cleared away and was rebuilt in the form of a two-story Palladian pergola.

Morristown, New Jersey was home to the very rich at the turn of the century; it was located in the country, which was good for raising a family, and it was in close proximity to New York City for business. The Morristown Club was founded in 1884 by a group of millionaires. Kahn, despite his wealth and influence, was refused membership into the prestigious club and was blacklisted for all society events because he was Jewish.

Although he was born into the faith, his family in Germany never had strong religious beliefs, and rarely practiced Judaism let alone preached it. Throughout his life Otto Kahn contributed to Jewish causes as well as to Catholic and Episcopal charities, and in fact raised his own children in the Episcopal Church.

The Kahns spent less and less time at the Morristown estate, and Otto rented and purchased various other homes in the eastern United States and in Europe, one of them being St. Dunstan's mansion, acquired from the Earl of Londesborough in England. Still resentful of the harsh treatment he and his family was enduring in Morristown, Otto contemplated moving permanently to England, a "less anti-Semitic society." The English loved Kahn and even tried to get him to run for Parliament, but he had no aspirations for political office, and decided to go back to America. In 1915, Kahn offered to let the British Government use St. Dunstan's as a hospital for soldiers blinded in World War I. This continued until 1923, when Kahn sold St. Dunstan's.

Through the years, Otto Kahn amassed considerable wealth. He had come to America during the Gilded Age, when fortunes could be made overnight and there were no income taxes. Kahn had gained his fortune on his expertise in the banking field, and went on to be a builder of railroad empires, where he served on many boards. However, he was not obsessed with wealth and power. Kahn was a successful author and lecturer, and donated much of his time and money to charities and to the arts. He was respected by ordinary people as well as the wealthy. Otto Kahn openly supported Theodore Roosevelt's run for the Presidency, and the two became very close friends, with Roosevelt often seeking Kahn's counsel. When Roosevelt died in 1919, Kahn was deeply affected. Two years earlier, Kahn had become an American citizen, taking the Oath of Allegiance.

Kahn continued to purchase and develop properties in the United States. He had a plan for what was to be his greatest building achievement. The site he chose for his new home was on Long Island, in the area of Cold Spring Harbor known today as Cold Spring Hills. In

1914, Kahn purchased a 443-acre site there, and three years later Oheka Castle was nearly completed.

Kahn wanted his home to be situated on the highest point of Long Island. Many believe that his motivation was to prove to the people of Morristown that he could not be put down. Unfortunately, the highest point on Long Island was not available to Kahn, so instead he decided to build his own man-made mountain. For two years, hundreds of workers hauled dirt from the surrounding acreage on horse-drawn wagons. At the very top of the hill, his house would be built.

Otto Kahn loved large palaces, and he began thinking of ways to create his own. He hired a prestigious New York City architectural firm, Delano and Aldrich. A magnificent French chateau was suggested, and Kahn was delighted with the idea. Elsewhere on the property, there would be room for spacious formal and informal gardens, including reflecting pools, a greenhouse complex, a stable complex, swimming pools, tennis courts, an eighteen-hole golf course, and even a private air strip. Kahn's greenhouses alone, costing over one hundred thousand dollars to build, became one of the largest private nurseries in the United States. Since the Kahns loved gardening and the outdoors, it was their intention to decorate the house with fresh flowers everyday, year round.

To Otto Kahn, the house and the rest of the property, mainly the gardens, were of equal importance. He hired a famous and respected firm of landscape architects, Olmsted Brothers of Brookline, Massachusetts. Its founder, Frederick Law Olmsted, had been responsible for the landscaping of New York City's Central Park, the Capitol grounds in Washington, DC, and Vanderbilt's "Biltmore" mansion in Asheville, North Carolina. Kahn gave Olmsted Brothers permission to move as many trees, shrubs, plants, statues and fountains as they saw fit, from his Morristown home to Cold Spring Harbor. Kahn continued to work closely with both the Olmsted Brothers and with Delano and Aldrich, until America became involved in the First World War.

Construction, mainly on the gardens, was greatly slowed down at this point and eventually came to a complete standstill, with many of the workers going off to war. The Kahns also had to deal with the criticism of the neighbors, who were shocked by the continuation of an expensive private project during wartime. By December of 1918, one month after the armistice that ended the war, the project was once again slowly underway.

The Gilded Age had come to an end, and the Kahns decided to trim the development of the estate dramatically. Nevertheless, Kahn's new home and gardens were still impressive. He named the 126-room mansion "Oheka Castle." Otto Kahn loved symbolism and took his initials to form the name: **Otto HE**rmann **KA**hn (pronounced Oh-hee-kah). The house has 109,000 square feet of living space, making it the second largest private residence in the United States, with Biltmore being the largest. Often compared to San Simeon's Hearst Castle in California, Oheka is almost twice its size.

Oheka Castle, viewed from the front

The main entrance to what was Kahn's original estate can be seen today on Jericho Turnpike. The stucco turreted building that once served as the gate house is now a real estate office. The main drive takes you past Norway maples and Otto Kahn's famous golf course, now the Cold Spring Harbor Country Club. Continuing past the golf course, one approaches a pair of hand-wrought iron gates built into a Norman-style tourelle, containing a narrow circular staircase leading from the entrance circle to what once was an upper rose garden. Although the garden is gone, the structure and entrance gates remain.

Heading toward the main house, there is an entrance tower and another tourelle, capped by a multi-family birdhouse and weathervane; it also contains a circular staircase that leads to the main terrace. The driveway is over a mile long, and opens up into a large courtyard paved with cobblestones. When Oheka was built, it was decided that the main house would be enclosed by the courtyard on the north and west sides, and a retaining wall would separate the courtyard from

The indoor swimming pool

the servant's wing and yard on the east side. On the south side, a terraced balcony sitting area overlooks a terraced lawn. The main facade of the house runs the full length of the courtyard.

Below the terraced balcony is the indoor swimming pool, finished in marble and tile, and measuring over seventy-five feet in length. There are large sitting areas at both ends; surrounding them and the running the entire length of the pool are nine large Palladian windows. Magnificent ivy-covered vaulted arched ceilings are above. Outside the Palladian windows, Kahn had large linden trees planted. The linden tree was a symbol of Kahn's home town in Germany, and lindens were planted in various locations around the Oheka property.

Oheka Castle has three floors and a basement. The concrete, block and brick structure has sharply peaked slate roofs, and its towers and chimneys add another story to the mansion. The sills and quoins or corners of Oheka are all trimmed with limestone, and the basic shape of the house is a capital E.

Upon entering Oheka, one is greeted by the marble-floored Entrance Hall, which contains a magnificent horseshoe-shaped Grand Staircase surrounded by a double iron balustrade. The Grand Staircase leads to the balcony and Reception Hall located on the first level of the house. This main floor has been totally renovated by its present owner, Gary Melius. This area alone took three years to restore. A large gallery leads to the Library, Dining Room, and the Grand Ballroom, which measures seventy-two feet six inches by thirty-four feet five inches, with a ceiling height of almost sixty feet. On each end of the ballroom is a large fireplace, two of the thirty-nine fireplaces that exist throughout the house.

The Grand Ballroom

A mezzanine level is located between the main level and the second floor of Oheka, containing a small wing that was used by the estate's housekeeper. Eight other servants' bedrooms were located in another wing on this level. The second floor, when the Kahn family finally moved in, had thirteen master bedrooms, each with its own sitting room and fireplace, twelve master baths, and a large linen room. The third floor had five master bedrooms and baths, a school room, sewing room, twenty servants' bedrooms, several large cedar closets and a storage area. It is said that at one time Kahn had as many as 125 servants working and living in his house.

French chateaus were known for having secret rooms and passageways, and Oheka was no exception. Otto Kahn had a secret room built off the Library, complete with a revolving bookcase. A center panel in the bookcase was fitted with hinges which would swing open when touched to reveal a narrow passageway leading to a secret room that Kahn said was his secretary's office. That room is now a lavish ladies room.

The Library, where a secret room is hidden behind a bookcase

Besides the secret room, it is also said that Otto Kahn had secret tunnels built from the main house to the Cold Spring Harbor train station, and another tunnel which led to the harbor. Mr. Kahn had a large yacht also called Oheka, that he used to pick up guests from the city and bring them back to the harbor, where a car would be waiting for them at the tunnel to whisk them back to the castle. There is no proof that these tunnels were ever built, but according to Eastern Military Academy, which occupied the building from 1948 to 1978, the tunnels did exist but were cemented shut and used as a target range.

Another strange area of the house is the basement, where cage-like rooms can be seen. Rumors abounded that Kahn kept wild lions and tigers in these cages to guard the castle and the estate from intruders. These structures exist today, but they were in fact built as wind tunnels; they created fresh air passages for Kahn's sophisticated air conditioning system, which extended up through the basement and cooled the entire house. Kahn also had a complete power generator and a water pumping station in the basement, so he did not have to rely on others during a power failure.

The wind tunnels, once thought to have been lion's cages.

Otto Hermann Kahn suffered a heart attack and died on March 29, 1934, while having lunch in the private dining room of Kuhn, Loeb and Company. He was sixty-seven years old, and left behind four children, Maud, Margret, Gilbert Wolff and Roger Wolff. Funeral services were kept simple, and were held in the music room of Oheka. He was buried in the family burial plot in Cold Spring Harbor.

Oheka Castle remained vacant until 1939, when the estate was purchased by the New York City Department of Sanitation for use as a weekend retreat for its 15,000 members. This usage, however, was against the Town zoning laws, and it was quickly shut down.

By 1948, the castle and approximately 23 acres of the 443-acre estate, including the mansion, were sold to the Eastern Military Academy. One hundred and fifty acres of Kahn's golf course became the Cold Spring Country Club, Kahn's greenhouses on six acres became the Otto Keil Florist, and the remaining 264 acres were used to develop 300 residential homes in the community of Cold Spring Hills.

Unfortunately, during the time the Eastern Military Academy occupied the site, further renovations to suit their needs took place, and the once magnificent gardens were bulldozed over. By 1978, the school went into bankruptcy and Oheka Castle was left abandoned. It was severely abused by vandals, until Gary Melius purchased it in 1984. Mr. Melius has spent over $12 million dollars restoring Oheka. In 1989, he sold the castle to a Japanese trust, but retains a ninety-nine year lease.

Although the Otto H. Kahn estate as been the subject of some debate and criticism over its usage, one thing is certain: the beautiful Oheka Castle has been saved, restored and preserved for all generations to come. The Town of Huntington should take great pride in the magnificent home that has seen the likes of singer Enrico Caruso, conductor Arturo Toscanini, movie actress Helen Hayes and entertainer Fanny Brice. The massive edifice was even used in Orson Welles' "Citizen Kane," but perhaps the most important person to remember is the man who built the castle on the hill — Otto Hermann Kahn.

(For further information on Oheka, I recommend *Raising a Fallen Treasure: The Otto H. Kahn Home, Huntington, Long Island,* by Robert B. King. It served as a valuable source of information for this story.)

ST. JOHN'S EPISCOPAL CHURCH

If one is traveling to Oyster Bay from Cold Spring Harbor's Route 25A or by way of Route 108, a familiar and most beautiful landmark is passed. Through every season, the quaint little white church by the pond looks as if it just popped off the pages of some New England magazine. St. John's Episcopal Church has been a wonderful part of Cold Spring Harbor's past. Overlooking the salt meadows and harbor, the spire of this historic church became a home-town greeting, welcoming whalers back from a long journey at sea over one hundred years ago. It is a place people have visited, photographed, and keep coming back to. I myself recall wonderful days spent there as a child, where my family and I walked around the pond and fed the many ducks, swans and geese. For others, winter brought a new pastime. Like something from a Currier and Ives print, bundled-up skaters could be seen gliding over the icy pond.

Many people have special memories of St. John's Episcopal Church, which has a history that dates back more than 160 years.

From 1800 to 1831, Episcopalians living in Cold Spring Harbor worshipped in a small red school house built in 1790, located not far from the present church. On September 4, 1831, the members of the small congregation got together and decided it was time to build a church. John H. Jones agreed to sell three-quarters of an acre to the parish, providing that, "No other building other than a church for the Protestant Episcopal society shall ever be built ..." Shortly thereafter Mr. Jones died, but his heirs agreed to sell the land for $200. Records indicate that the land was located "at the end of the lower mill dam on the edge of St. John's Lake, overlooking the salt meadows and the harbor." This purchase also included adjacent land near the sand bank, which would be used for building a carriage shed.

Money still had to be raised, however, for the building of the church. Sixty-nine subscribers pledged between $1 and $200, and soon $2,279 was raised. The architect and builder of the church was Smith Sammis, who constructed the church in 1835 at a cost of

$3,215. The Reverend Isaac Sherwood served as first rector, and Simon Rice was appointed sexton. On October 5, 1836, St. John's Church was incorporated in the Queens County courthouse, and on April 5, 1837, Bishop Benjamin Treadwell Onderdonk from the Diocese of New York consecrated the building and "thereby separated it from all unhallowed and common uses and solemnly dedicated it to the holy purposes above mentioned."

The little white church, with its plain glass windows, was built in a New England colonial style, and did not originally have a steeple, only a square base for one. Not long after, the vestry voted to erect a steeple and cross. The spire soon became a symbol of home, welcoming sailors back from the sea. Outside the church, two front doors, one for ladies and one for gentleman, opened into two aisles on the outside of two columns of square pews. The pews had doors which opened on each end, and from them hung brass nameplates indicating the owner of the pew. The money which was collected from the renting of the pews was applied toward the salaries of the rector and the sexton. The sexton also earned $1.75 for each grave he dug.

There was no chancel, so the altar, which was surrounded on three sides by a communion rail, was on the same level as the pews and stood where today's steps are located. The church was heated by two large wood-burning stoves, and the church bell was given to the parish by the women who "earned the money by sewing and having sacrificed thimbles and other silver, that their church bell should have a silver peal." By 1839, the first rectory was purchased from Divine Hewlett.

During the mid 1800's church styles began to change from colonial to neo-Gothic. At the same time, St. John's received a new rector, Reverend Edward F. Edwards, and he began making changes to the church. Between 1851 and 1871, the interior walls and ceiling of the church were painted olive green, stenciling was added, and the woodwork throughout the building was stained darker, in order to represent real English oak. Another rectory was acquired, along with additional land for the Memorial Cemetery and the cemetery chapel. The rectory had been the home of miller Lewis Seaman, and was given to the parish by members of the Jones family. In 1864, land was also given south of the church in order to build a recess chancel. The younger members of the Jones and Hewlett families furnished the new chancel and donated a larger altar, a carved cross, new furniture, a large pulpit, choir stalls and "silverized" candlesticks.

When a new rector, Reverend Robert Howard, came to St. John's in 1871, the church building underwent further changes, including restaining the pine pews in their natural wood color, creating three aisles to the church instead of two, and closing off the vestibule. A bellows organ, which had been built by Henry Pilcher of Brooklyn in 1847, was replaced with a new organ, gift of the Hewletts, and was installed in the southwest end of the church. Soon afterwards, the first three memorial stained glass windows replaced those of clear glass. (It is unknown where the beautiful Tiffany windows came from, but they are thought to have been installed sometime after 1900.)

The interior of St. John's Church was repainted and re-carpeted once again at the turn of the century. The old

St. John's Episcopal Church in Cold Spring Harbor

wood burning stoves were replaced, the organ was repaired, and electric lights were installed. Reverend William E. McCord accepted the position as new rector of St. John's in 1919. Renovations and improvements continued inside the church, and the Rectory, which was greatly in need of expansion and repair, also became a primary project. It was at this time that a Parish House was added, at a cost of $6,000.

The road which once ran directly in front of St. John's and across the mill dam was closed to the public in the early 1900's. The new road, running between Oyster Bay and Huntington, was relocated further north across the salt meadow at the head of the harbor. The original white fence which had separated the front of the church from the road was taken down, and the road was filled in and planted with grass.

Reverend McCord's stay at the parish did not last long. He resigned the same year he came, to sail overseas with the men who were on active duty in France, with New York's Seventh Regiment. He felt his obligation was to his calling as a chaplain. Dr. Ralph Wood served as interim minister until Reverend Harry Barrett accepted the rector position in 1919 until about 1930.

In 1931, Reverend Lyman Cox Bleeker from Connecticut accepted the rector's position, which he held for thirty-two years. The church was again in need of repair and refurbishing, but this was not the only problem. Attendance on Sundays had greatly declined. Many other old wooden Episcopal churches in need of repair, were torn down, but Reverend Bleeker valued the beauty and simplicity of the historic little church. Within a year, he had the interior of the church painted in cream tones, installed a new heating plant, and re-wired the entire building. Four beautiful new chandeliers replaced the single one, and were given to the church by Mrs. Walter Jennings.

About this time, the church was fortunate to acquire the additional ten acres and pond that adjoins the churchyard to the east. The site had once been the location of a working mill, which had burned down some years before, and the pond had been sold to Robert W. de Forest. When de Forest died in 1933, the pond was offered to the church for $25,000. The vestry could not raise that much money and had to decline the offer. Mr. de Forest's sons offered to contribute $10,000, and the estate agreed to let St. John's have it for an additional $10,000. The church raised $6,000 in voluntary contributions, while the Jones family came up with the rest, through a balance owed by a legacy given to the church by Mrs. John O. Jones some years before.

In 1936, Sarah Elizabeth Jones and her sister Florence Loretta gave their birthplace, the family home which was built in 1698, to the church. It serves as the rectory today. The church went through a series of changes again during the 1940's. A second pulpit was built to enclose the brass lectern, a canopy was erected over the altar, and a dossal curtain was hung from it to cover the stained glass window, which had caused excessive sun glare. By 1949, St. Michael's Church in Brooklyn had given pews to St. John's; they were placed in the balcony. More land was donated to the church by the Wawapek Society, and was used to create the lower parking area.

Interestingly enough, during World War II, because of gasoline rationing, the 9 o'clock and 11 o'clock services were combined into one service at 10 o'clock. Two buses were hired to transport parishioners to and from the church, and it is said that they often stopped for ice cream on the way home.

Once the war ended, change came to Long Island and many new homes were built. There was an enormous increase in church membership, and by 1950, something had to be done to accommodate the ever-growing Sunday School. The church building was moved onto fill at the corner of the pond, so that the original Parish House could be extended eastward. The Jones monuments were then placed on either side of the entrance, and ten feet was added to the south end of the chancel to provide more room for the choir. St. John's continued services during these changes, despite the church being on stilts.

Enrollment continued to increase, so there still was not enough room in the tiny church. Finally, in 1962, a new two-story building with an adjoining outdoor chapel was built and dedicated on property to the west and south of the church, which had once been the Arthur Jones property. Church membership included 700 families by this time, with 425 children registered in the Sunday School. That same year Reverend Bleeker announced his retirement. A portrait of him was unveiled in his honor at the dedication of the new building, which was appropriately called Bleeker Hall. Bishop James P. de Wolfe had the privilege of taking part in the dedication and unveiling. Reverend Bleeker had contributed forty-nine years of religious service at St. John's Church.

The Reverend T. Carleton Lee served as rector from 1963 until 1993, when Reverend Churchill G. Pinder, its present pastor, arrived to replace interim rector William H. Hale in 1995. Born in Virginia, Reverend Pinder and his wife came to St. John's from All Saints Episcopal Church in Portland, Oregon.

The charm and tranquillity remains today in the quaint, historic St. John's Church. Now and in the years to come it will continue to attract both visitors and parishioners, who see this local landmark as an important part of Cold Spring Harbor's beauty and history. It remains for both people, and wildlife, to enjoy.

THE TREASURES IN THE ATTIC OF CAPTAIN SAMUEL T. MITCHELL'S HOME

History is revealed to us in many ways. Old records, files, books, magazines and even movies are good sources for historic information, as are interviews with people who played a part in past events — people I call "living history." Recently I was fortunate to discover yet another way of going back in time. During an interview with Vivian and Andrew Mathews, residents of Turkey Lane in Cold Spring Harbor, I had the rare opportunity to enter a place people read about in books. I was invited into the old darkened, third-floor attic in what had once been the home of the seafaring Captain Samuel T. Mitchell. It was there that some fascinating history was revealed to me.

The sources and contacts for the places I research come to me in many ways, and through many interesting people. Elected to the Huntington Historical Society Board of Trustees in August of 1996, I meet a lot of people sharing an interest in history — many of them, like myself, living in an older home. It was Vivian Mathews, also a Board member, who told me about her home, where an old sea captain had once lived. I of course followed through, and set up an interview to see and discuss the history of the house. Exactly one week before Halloween, on a windy Thursday night, I sat in the kitchen of the Mathews home and listened to their fascinating stories. The Mathews are too young to be "living history;" instead, they passed on what they had been told. Then we ventured into ... the attic.

The residence on Turkey Lane has an interesting background. This two-bay, 2½ story gable-roofed house was built in 1877 for Captain Samuel Mitchell, a whaler and later a coaster, who sailed his famous vessel the *Eliza J. Raynor*. The house reflects the Gothic Revival style,

Captain Samuel Mitchell's House

with its gingerbread exterior trim and double pointed attic windows. Originally the house had a porch and shutters, both of which rotted away and were removed sometime during the 1950's. The Mathews have obtained replacement shutters that they plan to put up, and hope one day to be able to replace the beautiful porch that once existed there. The house stands one lot south of the historic district boundary of Cold Spring Harbor, in a residential sector of that district.

According to Cold Spring Harbor Whaling Museum records, Samuel Mitchell came to Cold Spring Harbor from Martha's Vineyard in 1861, and had the house built for himself and his wife several years later. Although his home was in Cold Spring Harbor, Mitchell continued to command whaling and commercial vessels from various ports.

The Mathews showed me many photos of the house during the Mitchells' occupancy, that were either given to them or found in the attic. One photo shows a girl and a dog standing on the porch. The Mathews were told the girl was Aida, the Mitchells' adopted daughter. The Mitchells had no children of their own, and when the Captain's first mate died at sea, leaving a young daughter, the Mitchells decided to adopt her. Supposedly, Aida was from England.

Aida grew up in the house and inherited it from her adoptive parents upon their deaths. It is unclear when Mrs. Mitchell died, but Samuel Mitchell died in 1906. Aida married Oliver Schultz, and the two continued to live in the house and raised a family there.

According to Andrew Mathews, Schultz sold the house to a John A. Gardner, date unknown, and Gardner sold the house to Mrs. Gilbert Ball in 1954. Mrs. Ball sold the house to the Mathews in 1991, making the Mathews the fifth owners of the house. Further research indicated that in 1917 someone by the name of Holmes owned the house. However, nothing is known about who Holmes was or how long he lived there. The name appeared on a Building-Structure Inventory Form from the Huntington Historical Society in 1979.

When the Mathews purchased the house from Mrs. Ball, they were told many stories, not about the previous owner, John Gardner, but about the Schultzes. Mrs. Ball had owned a book store in Cold Spring Harbor for almost forty years, and grew very fond of an old woman who frequented her store. The old woman happened to be Mrs. Aida Mitchell Schultz. They became friends, and Mrs. Schultz, knowing that Mrs. Ball was living in her old house, gave Mrs. Ball old books, photos and of course, information. Mrs. Schultz explained that the small room located on the second floor (window to the left in photo on p. 17) was at one time the local telephone exchange for the area. Her husband Oliver ran the local telephone company, and for convenience sake had the exchange put in that room. According to Mrs. Ball, one of the houses connected to the exchange was Sagamore Hill, the home of President Theodore Roosevelt.

Mrs. Gilbert Ball had an interesting story herself, which was told by her granddaughter during a visit to the house after the Mathews had purchased it. "We had owned the house for about two years," Vivian Mathews told me, "when there was a knock at the front door. A woman was standing there and told me she was the granddaughter of the Balls, and that she was a college professor from Ontario. I invited her in and we sat at the kitchen table and talked, and had some tea.

"She told me the Balls had been lovers," Vivian continued. "Gilbert Ball left four children and a wife in Sag Harbor back in the 1940's to marry Mrs. Ball, who was single. They never had any children of their own. This [house] was their love nest. When we moved in, Mrs. Ball was very old, and she had left a lot of things behind. Her wedding picture, showing her in her dress in this room, was lying on the floor along with some negatives. Well, when her granddaughter went on to tell me that her grandfather, Gilbert Ball, was buried in the backyard. I almost dropped my teacup!"

Obviously, in the twentieth century, human bones could no longer be buried in one's yard, so it is assumed that Gilbert Ball was cremated and his ashes were either scattered or buried in the backyard. Vivian and Andrew recalled a statue of a Buddha in the middle of the yard, when they first looked at the house. Mrs. Ball said she was planning on taking the statue with her when she moved. Perhaps this was where Mr. Ball's remains went.

Vivian had been living and working in London, where she and Andrew Mathews met and married. They decided to buy an old house back in the United States, and Cold Spring Harbor proved to be just the place. Despite its need for substantial updating, the Mathews fell in love with the charm of the Samuel Mitchell house, with its original hand-blown glass windows, original moldings, hardwood floors, and the interesting curved wall on both the first and second floors.

Andrew Mathews then related the following strange event to me.

"We heard that the house had just come onto the market the day the real estate agent took us to see it. When we went back outside, knowing we loved the house, she said, 'Would you like a picture of it?' and I said, 'Sure.' She said, 'Well, here's a Polaroid camera; why don't you go across the street and take a snapshot.' So I found the best angle, lined it all up and took the picture. The Polaroid shot out and slowly developed, and we saw the house appear. We were studying it and Vivian said, 'Andrew, I can see a lady staring out of the window upstairs.' I looked at it, and yes, you could see a Victorian lady wearing a hat, looking out the window."

Although they don't exactly believe in ghosts, there was no denying that both Mr. and Mrs. Mathews saw a woman appear in the photo. In fact, sometime later Vivian showed her grandfather the photo of the house, and mentioned nothing about what happened the day it was taken. Her grandfather immediately asked who the woman was in the upstairs window. (To my dismay, no one unusual appeared in the photo I took of the house in the fall of 1996).

The Mathews did show me the Polaroid taken in 1991, and only a faint outline of a woman now appears, since the photo has greatly faded over the last several years. "If it was a ghost, it welcomed us and left us alone," laughed Andrew, claiming they never heard the sound of clanking chains.

Another unusual occurrence took place when the Mathews were updating and renovating the kitchen, the biggest undertaking in the house so far. One night Vivian heard what she called "old fashioned songs" being sung, music she did not recognize. Thinking it was probably just a dream, she dismissed the incident. A year or so later, while watching a television show about whaling times and sailors, she heard the unfamiliar songs and learned that they were old sea chanteys. It certainly makes one wonder.

Now, what was in the attic of this interesting old house? Before we went up, the Mathews showed me a book they put together on the house, containing many old photographs. As mentioned, the Mathews obtained many things from Mrs. Ball, including the photographs of the Mitchells that Aida Mitchell Schultz had given her. Besides the photo of Aida as a child on the front porch, an earlier photo appears with an older woman standing on the front steps. Perhaps this is Mrs. Mitchell. Another photo of the house shows an old hitching post which was used to tie up horses in the days before cars. Most fascinating of all were two photos of Mrs. Mitchell taken in the house. In one 8 x 10 photo she was wearing in a long black dress, and was seated with her hand on a nearby chair. The chair was one of ten antique chairs that the Mathews found in the attic. The other photo, a smaller picture, was of Mrs. Mitchell wearing another long dress, standing by the fireplace in the living room. A parlor chair appears in the photo. That too was found in the attic.

The fireplace that appears in the photo was not a working fireplace, but was used for decoration instead. The Mitchells used a more modern means of getting heat by having pot bellied stoves throughout the house, none of which exist today. The decorative mantle still remains in the Mathews living room, however.

When the Mathews moved into the house, Mrs. Ball had given them a small gold decorative box that opens like a book. It contains a very small oval tintype of a young Captain Samuel Mitchell. He didn't have a beard in this photo. However, in the Mathews album is an 8x10 tintype taken later; it has a hint of hand-coloring, and shows Captain Mitchell with a long beard.

Other items in the album are photos of Cold Spring Harbor and of the first Cold Spring Harbor school house, as well as copies of signed letters written by Captain Mitchell. The originals can be found at the Cold Spring Harbor Whaling Museum.

After we looked through the photographic history the Mathews had put together, they gave me a tour of the house. Then we went up past the narrow wooden door, and climbed the steep winding steps to the dimly-lit unfinished attic.

Once dubbed Nancy Drew by an author friend of mine, I felt I was living out my childhood dream of roaming through someone's mysterious attic. Vivian and Andrew showed me items from all time periods.

Andrew waved yellow banners with "I Vote For Women" written across them, while Vivian showed me hundreds of old books and bibles. The oldest book found in the attic was a supply log book from a whaling ship dating from the late 1700's. This could not have been Captain Mitchell's, obviously, but it may have come from Mrs. Ball's old book shop. Andrew showed me an old opium pipe and case he found in the attic; he doesn't know whose it was or where it came from. I saw one of the antique chairs, and the parlor chair from the photo, in need of repair. Other items included an old sewing machine and thread, luggage tags that say "To Europe" on them, and a photographic album of a couple's tour around Europe, circa 1930.

The items found belonged to the Mitchells, the Schultzes and the Balls. The most evocative thing in the old attic probably belonged to Mrs. Mitchell, because of its age and style. There, hanging on a rod, was a long, black Victorian skirt and jacket. Was it the one worn by Mrs. Mitchell in the photo? Or was it the one worn by the ghostly figure that appeared in the Mathews' Polaroid picture?

As I walked down the winding attic stairs, Vivian and Andrew told me they contemplated finishing the attic and turning it into usable space. Seeing history come alive in this timeless, rustic attic of the Mathews' home, all I could say was that I'd keep it just the way it is.

LUCIEN HILL:
FISHERMAN, OUTDOORSMAN, PRESIDENTIAL BODYGUARD

It was raining the day the tall, reserved man of eighty years came to my door, seemingly unaffected by the unusual weather conditions we were having for a January morning. He entered and quietly tipped his hat in a friendly yet formal hello. He was Mr. Lucien Hill of Cold Spring Harbor, and he was here to tell me about his life in his favorite little town by the sea.

As we sat drinking coffee and watching the rain come down in torrents, we spoke a bit about Short Hills, New Jersey where Mr. Hill grew up, and finally what brought him, or shall I say, drew him to Huntington and to Cold Spring Harbor. He was about nineteen years old when he began working in New York City for a large real estate firm called Previews, Inc., where he did mostly estate work, including settlements, appraisals, and promotional work for luxury homes. These homes happened to be right in the heart of the North Shore's Gold Coast. Eventually, Mr. Hill became an independent agent located on 38 New Street in Huntington and sold such places as the Noyes Estate on Woodbury Road, which was his biggest sale as a young man. Another of his favorite sites was the old Fairchild place on Shore Road in

Cold Spring Harbor. It contained an original bar left over from the whaling days.

According to Mr. Hill, one of the best parts about being involved in real estate was how he was able to spend his free time. "I was probably the only real estate man around traveling with a fishing rod and some lures in his car," he said. "When there was time off I'd always go fishing. I am a fisherman at heart; it's my real love in life—that and bird shooting, pheasant shooting and dog training."

Lucien Hill

Mr. Hill went on to explain, "Ever since I was old enough to pick up a fishing rod and a gun I was interested in fishing and hunting. In real estate I worked weekends and there was no golfing or tennis for me, so I hunted and fished during the week."

When World War II broke out Lucien Hill went off to war on December 27, 1941. Later he became a Military Policeman, spending about eight months as President Franklin D. Roosevelt's bodyguard.

"Due to my size — I'm 6 foot 4 — I was picked out of the outfit down in Fort Jay, Governor's Island, and wound up guarding President Roosevelt out at Hyde Park, New York—the summer White House where he spent a lot of time."

Sitting back in his chair, Mr. Hill recalled the only time he had made an arrest while working for the President. "Someone had wandered onto the property without any of us knowing about it. I saw this guy coming through the woods, so I grabbed him. Embarrassingly enough, it turned out to be the Secretary of the Interior, Harry Hopkins!" Hill laughed "He was fishing in the President's pond! He was swiping his trout!"

President Roosevelt was not the only prominent person Mr. Hill protected. He also served as the bodyguard to Holland's Queen Wilhelmina, Madame Chiang Kai-Shek and Sir Winston Churchill. Lucien Hill was discharged from the Army on August 25, 1945, and after taking a year off, he finally went back to a simpler life in real estate and of course ... fishing.

Shortly after, he married his wife Marianne, who shared Lucien's love of fishing and the Island, especially Huntington and Cold Spring Harbor.

"When I was living in New York but working on Long Island I remember passing through Cold Spring Harbor, Lloyd Harbor and Huntington, and I thought what a wonderful spot it was. Cold Spring Harbor was especially quiet and simple, and that's what attracted me to it. That and the proximity to the water. Main Street Cold Spring Harbor was much different from today."

"There was a small post office which is now a store," he remembered. "There was a little grocery store, and two gas stations, one on the corner of Goose Hill Road, and one on the corner of Shore Road." He paused again. "There was a small stationary store, a library where the SPLIA gallery is now, some art galleries, and I remember when the store Hitching Post came in. The parking lot which is there today was just an empty field."

In 1954, the Hills purchased their present home on Wawapek Road in Cold Spring Harbor, where they raised two boys, as well as seven Labrador Retrievers which Lucien used for hunting. Wawapek Road acquired its name from the Wawapek farm that once stood there. Marianne taught school at St. John's Church in Cold Spring Harbor for sixteen years, retiring in 1985, and Lucien continued to work in real estate but spent as much time outdoors as possible.

He purchased an eighteen-foot boat and traveled around Long Island Sound to Connecticut, Eaton's Neck and as far west as Matinecock Point, using nature as a guide to help him catch fish.

"I fish by watching birds. I don't troll and I don't bait fish except occasionally with live bunker chunks. I generally watch for a concentration of gulls and terns. When they bunch up and start diving, that means the blues have pushed the bait up to the surface."

"I remember one time there was so many blues, fourteen to eighteen pounders, and I was catching them as fast as I could get a lure in the water. I put some back, saved about seven, and after a while with the light tackle I was using my hands got so cramped that I quit. When I got to the dock I was tired as hell and the tide had gone out completely. I had to climb up a long ramp with all these bloody fish. I took them home, filleted them and took them over to Woodhull Road where I gave them to the people who made noon meals for the needy. Fishing hasn't been that way since, but I know they'll come back," Mr. Hill said with a smile.

Making some of his own rods and lures, Lucien Hill generally fished alone or with his wife, taking in the quiet of nature and his love for the water. He loved the challenge of the sport, too, and often anchored his boat by Buoy 15, a "hot spot" off Lloyd Neck.

When he wasn't fishing, Mr. Hill was hunting locally for ducks and pheasant. "When I first moved here," he said, "there were more wild pheasants and quail than I've ever seen anywhere else in the world. With all the building and the encroachment of the raccoons and foxes, the pheasants and the quail have vanished. The beginning of the end for the pheasants was when they began to cut and mow Jennings Field in Lloyd Harbor. That took away the cover needed for the pheasants, and the raccoons began to come. Today, Jennings Field is deeded to the Incorporated Village of Lloyd Harbor as long as it is kept cut and used for riding."

Further research showed that in December 1964, the heirs of Walter Jennings deeded to the Village a gift of fourteen acres. The conveyance was subject to the sole restriction that the property not be used for residential, commercial or industrial development except with the consents of the grantors or their heirs. In February 1965, another gift of 13 adjacent acres was given to the Village. The Village Board members decided to name the entire property "Jennings Field." In

1963, at the request of the owners of abutting properties, Huntington Road, within Village limits, had its name changed to Jennings Road.

Although certain things have changed in the Huntington area, Mr. Hill and his wife are content with the life they have made for themselves. For a person who hates to be indoors, Mr. Hill has enjoyed the time he has spent on the water, on the land and even in his own backyard growing flowers, vegetables and peaches.

Glancing once more at the rain falling lightly now outside my window, Lucien Hill put on his hat and coat and gave me a smile. I felt fortunate to have spent a few hours with him, learning about the essential simplicity of life, and how one man found everything he ever wanted or needed right here in Huntington. As he tipped his hat again and walked out the door, he turned to me and said, "If I had to say one thing about Huntington, it's that it's pleasant. I've really had a wonderful life here."

HUNTINGTON

YE OLD TOWN SPOT: TODAY'S VILLAGE GREEN

Today's Huntingtonians frequently drive past the Village Green, not realizing the important role this area played in the Town of Huntington's early development. In fact, the "Town Spot," as it was called, is where Huntington actually began.

In 1653, three English settlers from Oyster Bay, Richard Houldbroke, Robert Williams and Daniel Whitehead, purchased land from Chief Raseoken of the Matinecock Indian tribe. There were only thirty Indian families living along the shore at the time. They occupied the valley near the harbor, where their huts and wigwams were located. The number of Indians had been greatly reduced by a war with the Pequods of Connecticut, and by a pestilence that had swept over the Island long before the arrival of the English. Due to these circumstances, the Indians felt weak and vulnerable when approached by the English, and sold their land off very cheap.

The Indians made "wampum" (a form of money) from fragments of seashells. The English defrauded the Indians by learning how to manufacture their own "wampum" which they called "hard money." The result was that eventually the white men had all the land and the Indians had all the wampum.

The original purchase from Chief Raseoken, made on April 2, 1653, became known as "the Old First Purchase." The land stretched from what is now Cold Spring Harbor in the west, to Northport Harbor in the east, and from the Sound in the north to Old Country Road in the south. The territory was divided into 100-acre parcels, which centered around what was called the "Town Spot."

Of the three valleys around which Huntington grew, the broad eastern valley was chosen as the first village site because of its spring-fed stream, which still meanders through the Village Green. The "Town Spot" was the focus of the whole area. Houses were built around it, and it became a place to keep livestock, to vote, to buy things, to barter produce, and to hold town meetings. The area surrounding the "Town Spot"/Village Green is known today as the Old Town Green Historic District. The only surviving structure from this period is called Richard Latting's wing, c.1653, which is part of the 1702 Jarvis-Fleet House at Park Avenue and Woodhull Road.

The Huntington Village Green today

Huntington was often referred to as the wilderness. In some accounts of its earliest history, Huntington was known to have had deer, wolves, foxes, raccoons, otters, skunks and even bears. Wild fowl included turkeys, quails, partridges, pigeons, cranes and geese, while the waters off our shores teemed with whales and seals. There are two stories as to how Huntington got its name. Some believe it was originally called Hunting Town because of the vast numbers of wild beasts and fowl which could be hunted. More likely it was named after Huntington, England (later Huntingdon), the birthplace of Oliver Cromwell. Many of the early settlers were sympathetic to Cromwellian ideals.

The woods were sparse because they had been kept clear by the Indians prior to settlement, and the open land at the Green was one such spot. The settlers used the land first for planting, and then for keeping livestock, since cattle could graze and drink there.

Ten years later, however, it had become a nuisance to have the livestock running loose, so at a town meeting in 1663 it was decided the entire Green should be fenced in. The fence served a dual purpose. It made the town look neater, and it prevented the livestock from venturing out and being attacked by wild beasts or stolen by Indians. The Indians caught young wolves, tamed them and used them as dogs. These dogs became a great source of aggravation for the settlers.

During the day, some of the livestock would be driven to pasture at the "East Fields" later called "Old Fields" and then Greenlawn, and sometimes to the "West Fields," later called West Neck. At night, the entire stock would come together and be enclosed in the "Town Spot." Guards were set up to watch over the stock and the settlers' homes, and to keep them safe from Indians and wild beasts.

By 1659, the village had a dam built across the stream and a mill was constructed. By 1673, there were sixty-five families settled around the Green.

In the early 1700's, the Green or "Town Spot" was no longer enclosed. It contained only a small corral for stray animals. By this point, men had fenced in their own farms and built barns, stables and pens. The Green still retained a multitude of purposes, however.

The Huntington settlement rapidly grew in wealth and population. People gathered at the Green for meetings, where they discussed religion, school, Indian relations, shipping rights, trade and other aspects of daily living. Laws were made requiring every man to "provide himself with arms and ammunition for defense of the settlement- for the division of the lands- enclosing of fields- regulation of highways and watering places- for the destruction of wild beasts- collection of taxes-establishment and support of a school- for the prevention and punishment of crime- the preservation of good morals- the support of a minister."

The homes surrounding the Green were built by some of Huntington's earliest settlers, and housed a tailor, a hatter, a shoemaker, a tanner, a weaver, a brick maker, a mason, a victualler and a harness maker.

Several farms were also scattered about the area.

The Green was used as the parade ground for the Huntington Militia from the 1600's until the mid-1800's. During the British occupation of Huntington, the "Town Spot" was used by the King's troops as a camp ground and supply depot. When George Washington visited Huntington in 1790, its population was approximately 2,000, and by 1810 it had risen to over 4,000.

Eventually, as the middle and western valleys developed as commercial centers, the town Green diminished in importance. The earliest dwellings are gone, but the homes that do exist around the Green span the first three generations of colonial settlement within the town, and remain architecturally and historically significant.

As far as the Green is concerned, it retained its original land and configuration, plus some additional acreage at the north end which was added in the early twentieth century. The land today known as the Village Green is six acres, and is used as a town park. It has groves of trees, as well as the stream that originally attracted the settlers to the area. It remains a beautiful part of our town's history which can be appreciated and enjoyed by all.

HUNTINGTON'S OLD TOWN HALL

On the corner of Main Street and Stewart Avenue in Huntington, across from the Soldiers and Sailors Memorial Building, stands an authentic Colonial Revival building. The stately 2½ story brick structure has a slate hipped roof, flaring "U" plan and a monumental portico on colossal Corinthian columns. Round-headed windows are located on the second story under the portico, and a square deck clock tower with a hexagonal dome stands proudly on the top. Marble steps and a marble door enframement lead into the magnificent structure, which is both architecturally and historically significant.

When a need to house our Town's government arose in 1909, the prestigious New York City architectural firm of Peabody, Wilson and

Brown were engaged, and began drawing plans for Huntington's first Town Hall. They had designed several other public buildings in the Town of Huntington, including the Cold Spring Harbor Library and the Cold Spring Harbor Elementary School. However, it was their de-

sign for the Town Hall that was considered of exceptional architectural interest. It was featured in a professional journal called "Architect" in 1914, praising the firm and referring to the building as "a good example of Colonial Revival architecture." Throughout the eastern U.S. in the late 1800's there had been a revival of this type of architecture, said to have been

Huntington's Old Town Hall today

brought about by the Centennial of 1876. The facade of the old Town Hall is considered to be either of Georgian or Federal style. It was also one of the first Colonial Revival structures built on Long Island.

The building housed Huntington's government for 69 years. Prior to 1911, town meetings were often held in homes or at the Village Green. The first recorded town meeting took place on March 10, 1659, although the location is unknown. On December 7, 1663, a town meeting was held at "Goodman Finch's House," which stood somewhere on "The East Neck." By 1665, a "Meeting House" was built on the corner of Meeting House Path (now Spring Road), and Oyster Bay Path (Route 25A). The building was used both as a church and as a place for civic meetings until 1717. No other meeting place can be found in records until 1782, which mentions meetings held at the homes of Justice Platt, Esq., Widow Platt (on the corner of Park Avenue and East Main Street), Eliphalet Chichester in West Hills, and Platt Carll's house. From then on, Town trustees gathered at various places in Huntington, Northport and Babylon, to discuss village politics and problems. By 1872, the Eutropian Hall, which was located on the southwest corner of Main Street and New York Avenue, was used for discussion and debate. For several years Town meetings were held there, until 1909, when a larger and more permanent building was needed for the Town government. The population by this time was 12,004, and it became necessary to have larger accommodations.

There were several sites proposed for the first Town Hall, one being on the corner of Prospect and Main Street. Ultimately the land was provided by a public benefactor. The May 14, 1909 issue of *The Long-Islander* reported that: "*Dr. Oliver L. Jones has offered the town free of cost a site for the proposed new town hall on Main Street, just west of the Trade School. The site on the corner of Main Street and Stewart Avenue is the best location that could be named.*"

In an article dated May 28, 1910, *The Long-Islander* stated that "*Contractors Wanser and Lewis are making rapid progress upon the new town hall and it will probably be so that the town officials can move into it by the latter part of July.*"

When the building reached completion, the population was approximately 18,000. Not only were Town meetings held at the new location, but the new Town Hall also provided the first town-owned Court of Justice. A justice's bench was included as a necessary adjunct to the new building, and it served until December 31, 1965 when the position of Justice of the Peace was abolished. The first Justice to render a decision from the historic oak bench was the Hon. Justice Hendrickson, who presided there on November 5, 1910.

The bench was also used by the Town trustees and the Town Board, who conducted public meetings from it. The trustees' first meeting on the bench was held on November 4, 1910, while the Town Board, which was separate from the trustees, held meetings there until March 28, 1968. The method of rendering legal decisions changed in 1966, and the room and its equipment were no longer used as a courtroom. In March 1968, the old furniture was replaced with a modern semi-circular desk, which kept up with the changing times.

The bench was not the only interesting feature in the Old Town Hall. The clock tower had its own history. The clock, complete with four dials and an 800-pound metal bell, was given to the Town as a Christmas present by Miss Cornelia Prime, community activist and contributor to many area landmarks, including Huntington's first hospital. For fifty-five years the clock kept the time in the village until it was finally in need of repair and a new hand was installed. The original 24-inch long, wooden minute hand was given to the Town Historian in 1965, so it could be preserved in the town's archives.

Prior to 1910, many church bells rang on the Sabbath, and some tolled the hour. This tradition began during Huntington's early days, when an hourly announcement was given by the Town Crier. A drummer would announce the Sunday meeting hour. It is noted that the transition from drums to bells occurred in the early 18th century.

The first public timepiece was at the Central Presbyterian Church in Huntington Village and was dedicated on October 24, 1865. The three-faced clock struck every hour until it was destroyed by fire on September 12, 1888. As it fell to the ground, it tolled the hour of two a.m. In 1900, the Methodists built a tower with a three-dial clock on their Main Street church. That clock remained until 1954, when the church was torn down and a new one was built on West Neck Road. From that point on no other clock was built, since the Town Hall had such a beautiful and reliable one.

Just eleven years after it opened, the Town Hall could no longer accommodate the Town government, and in 1921 an addition was built. As the Town continued to grow, other government offices had to be set up in rented space throughout the Village. This situation lasted until 1978, when the space required had exceeded capacity.

The Town had no choice but to look for larger quarters. It was decided the old renovated school at 100 Main Street (its present location) would become the new Town Hall.

The beautiful old Town Hall went on the auction block on May 5, 1980, with the promise that the Town Board declare the site a historical area. Architectural features of the building could not be altered without the approval of the Town. The minimum bid was set at $200,000. The Huntington Chamber of Commerce and the Huntington Arts Council were both interested in using the building for office space, but the successful bidder was the Barrett-Treaty Corporation, an insurance underwriting firm.

Today, the building that once housed our Town government is serving the community in a new way. Signature Properties, Inc., A National Homefinder Company, is a real estate agency that finds people homes in Huntington. The Colonial Revival Town Hall is still a historical treasure, standing proudly as a symbol of bygone days.

THE TARRING, FEATHERING AND MURDER OF CHARLES G. KELSEY: HUNTINGTON'S MOST NOTORIOUS CRIME

On November 4, 1872 a crime occurred in Huntington which shocked not only the town but the entire nation. It began with the tarring and feathering of Charles G. Kelsey, a wealthy farmer/school teacher/poet, and ended in murder. Over 100 years have passed, and the murder and whereabouts of poor Kelsey still remain a mystery.

The story began with beautiful Julia Smith, daughter of the influential Smiths of Huntington. Julia lived with her grandmother, Charlotte Oakley, in a large clapboard house which once existed on Main Street near Spring Street. (The site is now occupied by an early 1900's home.) The only building that remains from the original property is an old red barn that was behind the house; it is located on Platt Place off Spring Road. It was at this site that the first of two crimes took place.

Charles Kelsey had fallen in love with the much younger Julia, and they were said to have had a brief romance despite Julia's engagement to Royal Sammis, a member of one of Huntington's most prominent families. Julia's family, hearing of the romance, greatly disapproved of Kelsey and told the girl to end the relationship immediately. A brokenhearted Kelsey continued to write letters to Miss Julia, which expressed both his anger and his love. Julia's grandmother intercepted many of the letters, so Kelsey went as far as to mail them by way of New York City. This lasted only a short time. Mrs. Oakley began to tell her friends and neighbors (especially Dr. George Banks), about the letters, calling them "obscene" and even accusing Kelsey of enclosing pornography. This was never proven. Some of the letters were given to local reporters, who called them "crazy utterances of a lovelorn idiot."

One of Julia's aunts, Abby Smith, was so suspicious of the letters that she decided to switch beds with her niece to see if Kelsey would come calling. Several nights later, while the aunt was sleeping, Kelsey is said to have entered the room through a window and attempted to make love to the aunt, who he believed was Julia. The aunt woke screaming and fled, locking the door behind her. When the aunt and grandmother went back to the room it was empty, and they surmised Kelsey had left via the window. This tale was never proven, but in Victorian days no one dared question a lady's word. The story was taken as truth, and so it lived on.

It was this tale that provoked the violence which would soon take place. It was the night of November 4, 1872, the eve of Grant's victory over Horace Greeley. The Democrats were holding a big rally and many of the local hotels were filled with visitors. Charles Kelsey attended the rally, and when it was over it appeared that Kelsey was on his way to his sister Charlotte's home, half a mile up Spring Street where Charles lived. But at some point he had arranged a secret meeting with Miss Julia. She was to give him a signal when the coast was clear, so he could come and see her. Unfortunately for Kelsey's sake, this was a setup, because his love had forsaken him.

Apparently Julia deliberately trapped Charles by waving the lantern in the cellar window, giving her former beau the signal to visit. (Later, in her testimony in front of a jury, Julia admitted that she lured

Charles with the lantern.) Upon his arrival, Kelsey encountered a band of masked men who jumped out from the backyard and stripped off his clothes. The men had been hiding beneath the branches of a willow tree, waiting for his arrival. Several of the men dragged out huge buckets of tar, while others brought large bags of feathers. In the barn, they cut off Kelsey's beard and hair, poured the buckets of hot tar over his nude body, and then covered him with feathers. Then the men dragged him to the front porch of the Oakley house, where Julia and her grandmother were waiting with some friends. A lantern was shone on poor Kelsey to prove, in the darkness, that it was in fact him. Enraged and humiliated, Kelsey lunged free, throwing his shoe at the lantern to extinguish it. However, one of the masked men grabbed the lantern and smashed Kelsey over the head. Finally, the men gave Kelsey his clothes back and he ran off to his sister's house.

The site of the tarring and feathering of Charles Kelsey

From this point on, exactly what happened remains a mystery. Charles G. Kelsey simply disappeared. According to his sister Charlotte, she found a tar-covered watch without a chain in the kitchen, and there were signs of a struggle on the front lawn.

The next day, Charlotte and two other brothers, Henry and William, began a search, but found nothing. Later that afternoon, a fisherman discovered a blood-soaked shirt on the shore of Lloyd Neck overlooking Cold Spring Harbor. The evidence was brought to the Kelsey brothers, who identified it as Charles's shirt. Setting forth their belief in his death, Henry and William brought the shirt and an affidavit to Justice of the Peace William Monfort. They claimed their brother was "the victim of foul and unlawful treatment," and an inquiry was opened in the village. Justice Monfort, based upon the Kelsey brothers' statement, charged Dr. Banks, Claudius B. Prime and Royal Sammis of riotous conduct and assault. The grave charges were sustained by the Grand Jury in a subsequent indictment.

Within days, all over the East Coast, Huntington was branded with the name "TAR TOWN." The little town became the target of every newspaper writer around, and the story spread nationwide when Kelsey's legs were found floating in Cold Spring Harbor.

The incident created great political problems in Huntington as well, for the once-quiet town was divided into "the Tars" and "the Anti-Tar" parties. The "Tars" were relatively small in number but were wealthy and influential, while the "Anti-Tars" opposed the outrage and held to the principles of law and order. This group was composed of many of Kelsey's friends.

It is said that even in his horrible condition, Kelsey recognized some of the masked men. Fearing exposure, the men may have followed Kelsey home, and under the motto "Dead men tell no tales," killed him. In the hopes of concealing their identity, the body was perhaps brought to the deepest spot in the harbor with weights attached, in the hope it would remain out of sight forever.

It was hard for many members of the community to believe that such respectable men could be involved. Some were sympathetic toward the men accused of the outrage, and claimed Kelsey deserved the punishment he got. They even believed that he was hiding out elsewhere in the United States, and that he would one day return to seek revenge on his enemies.

The Town was anxious to clear up the mystery, so Town Supervisor J. H. Woodhull offered a $750 reward for the production of the body of

Charles G. Kelsey, dead or alive. The reward was then increased by $500 by Kelsey's relatives.

Months went by with no sign of the body. In the meantime, Miss Julia Smith, seemingly unaffected by the event, married Royal Sammis in June 1873. Three months later, a grisly discovery would be made.

On August 29, 1873, fishermen John A. Franklin and William B. Ludlam were in two small boats in Oyster Bay, when they noticed something strange floating in the water. Upon closer inspection it appeared to be the lower portion of a human body. They fastened a line to it and towed it ashore, at which point they notified the Coroner.

The following passage is a quote from John A. Franklin at the opening of the inquest. (This material was taken from the book *The Kelsey Outrage*, published in Philadelphia by Barclay and Co. in 1873).

"While out in a small boat, midway between Plumb Point and More's Point, over what we call 'The Appletrees,' I saw a black object on the surface of the water, and as such sights were customary I did not pay any particular attention to it; I was about to draw my dredge, when my companion, William B. Ludlam, said, 'John, here is a body!' I pulled up my dredge and deposited it in the boat, and went towards Ludlam's; when I got close enough to see the object plainly, I said, 'It is nothing but a pair of pants!' Believing what I said to be true, I took hold of the pants and then discovered it was part of a carcass. 'Great God, John!' I said, 'it is a body, with nothing but the hipbones left!' I told Ludlum to tie a piece of string that was in the bow of my boat to the band of the pants, and secure it to the boat; he then said he would toss up with me to see who would tow it to More's Point; I said I would not, and told him to tow the body, and I would row ahead and go for the Coroner ...When the body was found it was covered with sea spiders."

Other witnesses were called to the stand, some of whom included Charles' youngest brother and the medical examiner. William S. Kelsey's testimony was important as to the identification of the legs. He recognized the remains as being that of his brother's. The legs had bits of tar and feathers on them, and he recognized the watch chain and comb which had been on the body. The chain had been in the Kelsey family for twenty years, and the comb was one carried by his deceased brother. The pants could not be recognized by William, but were later proved to be Charles' when his tailor had testified, and proved the work he had done on the pants.

A partial testimony revealing gruesome details from the medical examiner, Dr. M. Cory, appears below as it was written in the book *The Kelsey Outrage* (I have included this material so readers will understand the brutality of the crime).

"... I found that the parts were much decomposed; the bones of the pelvis on the inner side were devoid of flesh, but on the thighs there was a considerable amount which, although decomposed, was intact; the lower extremities were entirely denuded of flesh; on closer examination I found that parts of the anatomy between the pelvis and knees were missing;... I am of the opinion that it was the work of violence, and from the part that remains, think that the operation, if such was, was performed in a great hurry, thus leaving the part of which I spoke; the flesh from the lower extremities was, in my opinion, eaten by fish, for it presented a very jagged appearance, very unlike that of a body or part worn away or decomposed by the action of water; the remains of the missing part were not at all jagged, they being smooth and regular; the surface of the legs where there was most tar seemed to be better preserved than the other part not so well covered; I took two very large bundles of feathers from the part I spoke of, but they did not seem to adhere; I just lifted them off; I have not the means of knowing whether the black substance that I saw on the body was tar or not; in my opinion it was tar, but is not professional, and consequently unreliable; if the body had been in the water without weights it would have come to the surface in about a month or less, that being about the time that the gases take to generate; if the man committed suicide he would have come up at the time I speak of; if the body has been floating since December, I don't see why the other part is not there also."

Another doctor testified that the body was so terribly mutilated that it was a deed "expected from savages, not of peaceful Huntingtonians." He believed the body had been weighted down with ropes which were tied around the waist, and that the ropes were what cut through the torso.

The "tar crowd," despite the testimonies they heard, still argued that the legs were not Kelsey's, and that if they were, he had to have committed suicide. This did not stop Kelsey's family from having a funeral service for him. They accepted the remains for burial, believing it was Charles, and preparations were made. To make matters even worse, an unidentified person posted a horrible notice mocking the services to come:

N O T I C E

The funeral services of "Legs" will be conducted on Wednesday afternoon, at two o'clock, by the Rev. W. W. Knox, in the Presbyterian church of this village.

The services are expected to be deeply interesting, so much of "Legs" past and present history being known. A choir will be furnished for the occasion, composed of some of our greatest citizens, namely:

CHARLES DURYEA, alias Cyclops,
OLD GENERAL,
BIG BILL SAMMIS,
CHARLES STREET,
PETE TRAINER,

who will sing selections from "The Old Burying Ground," and "The Vale of Huntoria," etc.

Charles G. Kelsey may be present to entertain the assembly with some of his latest travels ...

The funeral at the Second Presbyterian Church was jam-packed. Never before had Huntington seen such a huge crowd gather for a funeral. It was a strange service indeed. The pastor would not permit the legs in the coffin to brought into the church. They were left outside on the lawn while services were going on. During a sermon, Charlotte Kelsey collapsed and was carried out of the church and into the crowd.

The remains were buried, but Huntington found itself the subject of bitter attacks in the nation's press. Finally, under the pressure of every major newspaper in the state, Governor John Dix in Albany sent his own aide-de-camp to Huntington to "clean up the mess." He offered a $3,000 reward, an unbelievable sum for the day, for the arrest and conviction of Kelsey's killers. The murder was considered one of the worst crimes of the century.

A coroner's jury continued to hear evidence at the courtroom in Oyster Bay in September through October. (Nassau was then part of Queens County, which had jurisdiction over Cold Spring Harbor. Coroner Valentine Baylis of Oyster Bay had ordered an inquest to determine whose legs were found and how they got there.)

Frederick Titus, a Negro servant in Royal Sammis' family, was a key witness. Under cross-examination he admitted that Sammis told him he was going to tar and feather Charles Kelsey. However, his memory seemed to fail shortly afterwards, and the same was true with the dozens of other witnesses who later took the stand. For years it was rumored that Titus never lacked a home or money to live on.

The jury made a decision on October 25, 1873, although it didn't accuse anyone specifically of homicide. It ruled the "legs" were definitely Kelsey's and that he "came to his death at the hands of persons unknown." It found that "Royal Sammis, George M. Banks, Arthur Hurd, William J. Wood, John McKay and Henry R. Prince aided, abetted, countenanced by their presence committal of the gross outrage and inhuman violence." They also ruled that Arthur Prime, Claudius Prime, S. H. Burgess, Rudolph Sammis and James McKay were "accessories before the fact."

The local newspaper, *The Long-Islander,* argued from the beginning that the legs were not Kelsey's, and that it was a conspiracy of local politicians and Kelsey's family to discredit some of the best families in town. They also insisted the trouble was being caused by New York City reporters who were "concocting their stories over the hotel bar."

The testimony was finally sent to the Grand Jury, forty miles away in remote Riverhead. On November 7, 1873, the grand jury indicted Royal Sammis and Dr. Banks for riot and assault, the original charges made against them when Kelsey disappeared. A few hours later the jury filed an indictment for second-degree murder against Royal Sammis and his brother Rudolph. The evidence provided by the district attorney for murder never showed up in open court. This too was a mystery.

Meanwhile, the fisherman finally received the $750 reward, but it cost Supervisor J. H. Woodhull his job. He lost the next election to Stephen C. Rogers, because an injunction was filed against him claiming the reward was illegal, despite the orders that had been given to him by the people of the town. He had prepared a special bill for the state legislature to make the payment. Woodhull not only lost the election, but was forced to pay the $750 from his own funds.

The Sammises and Dr. Banks tried to get their cases transferred to Supreme Court in Brooklyn (Kings County) on the grounds that they could not get a fair trial in Suffolk. By 1874 rumors arose that Charles Kelsey was alive and living in California. It turned out to be Charles' brother George, who had left Huntington twenty-five years before. Three years later, again in Riverhead, a jury hearing the evidence against Sammis and Banks returned a verdict of "not guilty." In October of 1876, Royal and Rudolph appeared in the same court demanding to be brought to trial or discharged. The District Attorney released both men in their own custody with the stipulation that they appear when ordered to. For reasons unknown, the order never came.

Royal and Julia Sammis, Dr. Banks and several other central figures in the case moved to New York City to live their lives in seclusion. Despite search after search, the upper body of Charles G. Kelsey was never found, and to this day it is not known who the murderer or murderers were. It will forever be a mystery.

THE PEOPLE AND STORIES BEHIND THE JARVIS-FLEET HOUSE

Many people in Huntington are familiar with the Kissam House on Park Avenue, owned by the Huntington Historical Society. Although you've driven past it often, you may not have noticed the big brown house just across Woodhull Street. The story of this house and the people who have lived there could probably fill a history book by itself. Known as the Jarvis-Fleet house, it is actually a very famous home, with the oldest section having been built in 1653.

The property on which the house sits was bought from the Matinecock Indians as part of the first Huntington purchase on April 2, 1653. Known as the area around the "Town Spot," the land was divided into individual deeded home lots, and was given to those settlers who contributed toward the purchase. It was Richard Latting, founder and "First Proprietor" of a 3½ acre tract, who owned and possibly built the oldest section of the house. The original one-room house was very small. It was 1½ stories high, and it contained a seven-foot wide fireplace that heated the ground floor room. The unheated loft above was reached by a winding staircase between the huge stone chimney on the west end wall and the front wall of the house. The beams of the house were made of rough-hewn logs. Many sources state that Latting built the original house, and others mention Richard Ogden, Latting's friend and neighbor, as the principal carpenter. Whatever the case may be, it was built in 1653 and is the oldest surviving structure in the Town of Huntington and central Long Island.

Richard Latting lived in the house until 1660, when apparently he was banished from the colony for "turbulent conduct." It is said that Latting, who appeared frequently in court records, violently opposed the settlers vote in favor of joining the Connecticut Colony for the purpose of protection against the Dutch. Latting moved to New Netherland, but still owned the Huntington house, then managed by his son Josiah. Eventually, the property was signed over to his son, who sold the entire homestead to John Robbins of Oyster Bay. Robbins immediately sold it to Huntington resident Richard Darling, who in turn sold it to a Mr. Benjamin Jones on March 3, 1669.

Jones lived in the house for only four years, selling it to a weaver, Joseph Wood, in 1673. Joseph had been raised in his parents' house just two doors down, and was among the first generation to be born in Huntington. Joseph Wood and his family remained in the old Latting house for almost thirty years, at which time he and his family moved to a farm on the south shore. On November 26, 1702 the house was sold to his brother-in-law, a whaler turned farmer, Captain William Jarvis. Jarvis had agreed to pay for the house, land and "Commonage" from the proceeds of one of his whaling expeditions. He owned thirty-eight small ships and was considered one of the wealthiest men in town. Jarvis immediately began construction on the little house. In the fall of 1702 a very large extension was added. Unlike the first section, Jarvis' addition was done by professional builders, with only the finest mate-

rials and craftsmanship. It is said the builders included his ship's car-
penters as well. All the beams were meticulously hewn by hand.

The 2½ story, five-bay, gambrel-roofed addition with 12-over-12
windows was completed during 1703, and transformed the structure
into one of the largest and most opulent homes in Huntington. Architecturally speaking, with its Georgian exterior, it was rather unique for
its time. It is one of the earliest known structures of English Gambrel
design to have a full two stories and an attic. It is the oldest example of
this formal plan still standing in the United States. The house had four
working fireplaces, one being set in a triangular fashion across a corner
of what was called the front parlor. The original pine paneling around
it is still intact. (Some other 18th century paneling from the Jarvis
house was sold in 1915, and is displayed in the Henry Ford Greenfield
Village Museum in Dearborn, Michigan.)

Jarvis-Fleet House (one-story wing at right side is original Latting home)

Captain Jarvis, who was also prominent in local politics, serving as
a Town Trustee from 1725 to 1731, lived in the house for over thirty
years. He sold the house to Joseph and Keziah Langdon, who in 1736
established the First General Store in Huntington, in the older (Latting) part of the home. Before the advent of the store, people in town

purchased various items directly from boats tied up at the Town Dock.

The Langdons lived in the main area of the house, keeping the store separate from the living quarters. They sold both to a Joseph Lewis, a saddle maker, on November 3, 1739. He extended the property and made the store into a leading gathering place and business. Lewis became the President of the Board of Trustees (mayor) for Huntington during the French and Indian War. His son, Joseph Lewis Jr., inherited the house in 1765, and took in a partner, Nathaniel Williams, to help run it. The Lewis family remained in the house throughout a very difficult time, the Revolutionary War.

Huntington was completely occupied by the British on September 1, 1776, who remained here until March of 1783. British and Hessian soldiers and officers took over many Huntington homes, including the Lewis house. In the fall of 1777, because of the size of the Lewis home and the number of fireplaces, a large contingent of British soldiers lived there until forts and barracks were constructed. Three town meetings even occurred there in December and January of 1777-78.

The Lewis family had no choice but to sleep in the loft of the old Latting wing, above the store. The British took siding and floorboards from the house and nails from the store, to build the barracks. At one point, Lewis's store was used as a cover for smuggling supplies to the Patriot Army in Connecticut by way of Long Island Sound.

In 1780, Joseph Lewis, Jr., like his father, was elected President of the Board of Trustees for Huntington, a position he held for only a year, since he died in 1781. His sons Joseph III and Richard Lewis became the owners of the (Jarvis) Lewis house, continued to run the store, and also became licensed innkeepers.

We finally see the Fleet name—probably the most famous of all who lived in the house—in 1793, when Samuel Fleet purchased it from the two brothers. Fleet added a two-story wing to the rear of the house around 1800, containing six rooms. This new addition made sixteen rooms in all. As for the little store, Fleet and a partner, Jesse Woolsey, successfully ran Lewis's business. All across Long Island, the firm of Fleet and Woolsey was quite well known. Besides the store, where he ran a post office and served as Postmaster from 1811 to 1823, Samuel Fleet was also an innkeeper, a founder of the Huntington

Academy, a partner in the Huntington Pottery, Town Supervisor in 1796 and Overseer of the Poor, among other things.

Samuel Fleet's son, Samuel Jr., became quite famous as well, succeeding his father in politics, and becoming the first principal of the Huntington Academy. He also became the founder and editor of Long Island's first magazine, *The Long Island Journal of Philosophy and Cabinet of Variety*, from 1825 to 1826.

Samuel Fleet, Sr. died in 1823, without a will and in debt. The house was sold in order to pay off his debts, and was purchased by Moses Scudder for one dollar. Moses did not live in the house, but instead rented it to a stonecutter named Phineas Hill, who set up his shop in an outbuilding located next to the house. Hill was the organizer of Huntington's first Methodist Church, and his son Francis was its first minister. While the church was being built, services were held in the stonecutting shop, while Mrs. Hill taught the first Sunday School classes in the house.

The Hills continued to live in the house until Moses Scudder's death, at which time it was sold to Samuel B. Keley, who shortly thereafter went bankrupt and liquidated all his holdings in 1846. Once again the house was for sale and was purchased by Brewster Skidmore, who moved the store to a different location. This move marked the end of 110 years of operation of the famous Huntington store. Skidmore lived in the house until 1857, when he sold it to the John A. Baldwin family, who owned it until 1871.

In the years to come, the house had many owners who used it as a boarding house. Some renovations were done in the late 1800's. By 1915, owner Janet Drake sold 34 acres of farmland, which had been part of the original property, for subdivision, and in 1916, had the large rear wing of the house removed.

During the Great Depression, the house was abandoned from 1936 until 1939, at which time plans were being considered to demolish it. Reginald H. Metcalf, (descendant of Michael Metcalf, the first free school teacher in the English colonies, teaching in Massachusetts in 1639), saw the value in the old home. Its interesting architectural features, its long history, and its sturdy foundation, were all reasons in

Metcalf's mind to save the old building. He rented the home first, in April of 1939, and finally purchased it in February of 1941.

Today the Jarvis-Fleet house is still owned by Reginald Metcalf, who has spent years restoring this wonderful and valuable piece of Huntington's history.

THE EARLY DAYS OF HUNTINGTON'S FIRE DEPARTMENT

It is not known how fires were fought prior to the 1800's, and before the establishment of fire departments. People probably tried to put out their own house fires, which may often have resulted in the house burning to the ground. Even when fire departments were beginning to form, the means for putting out a fire were quite primitive, despite having more manpower and some equipment. Nothing at that time could have compared to the ways in which fires are fought today.

By the early 1840's, as the population grew, there were numerous fires breaking out in Huntington Village. In 1843, concerned residents held a meeting to discuss forming a fire company to help protect the Village and its citizens. A group of volunteers formed the new company, bringing with them a few wooden ladders of their own, and leather buckets for carrying water. The men fought any fire in the Village which they could run to, or drive to in their buggies. Unfortunately, streams, wells, ponds and even cesspools were the only sources of water, and the range of extinguishment was as far as the strongest fireman could throw a bucket of water. As quickly as the buckets were filled, they were passed from hand to hand until they reached the fire.

In early 1846 a fire nearly destroyed the Old Huntington Academy, prompting a meeting of townspeople at the home of S.S. Scudder on January 23. They discussed the possibility of purchasing a fire engine "for the protection of life and property in Huntington Village." However, no means were found to raise the necessary funds, and the volunteers were forced to continue fighting fires with buckets.

In 1848, a local resident, Fayette Gould, became interested in the fire company, which by then was known as the "Protection Fire Company of Huntington." He and several other men joined the quickly growing company. By 1858, the company was reorganized and renamed the "Huntington Fire Company," with Fayette Gould elected first Foreman. Although the means for putting out the fires were basically the same, the water supply and equipment changed for the better just two years later. Beginning on September 18, 1860, measures were taken to purchase a hand pumper engine with money raised from public subscription. It was second-hand, having been built in 1845. Located in New York City, it had to undergo a complete overhaul before delivery. Meanwhile, on August 2, 1861 the first public fire well was dug on Main Street at a cost of $60. Locally, at the Leader's Carriage and Wagon Factory, a Hook and Ladder truck was built.

Eventually the rebuilt hand pumping engine was shipped via the Long Island Railroad to Syosset, which at that time was the end of the line. The engine was then towed by James Conklin's farm wagon to Huntington, where it was greeted by excited townspeople. Nicknamed "Masheen," the renovated engine was housed in a lean-to shed behind Zaphar Oakley's store. The first fire bell was also acquired around this time from the Old Huntington Academy. Eventually, the first firehouse was built behind George W. Conklin's Feed Store, which is believed to have been somewhere on or near Wall Street. The engine was housed there until the need arose to build a larger firehouse.

Another important year in the history of our firefighters was 1862, when the members of the Huntington Fire Company voted to apply for a charter from the State to incorporate. The Charter was passed by both the New York State Assembly and the Senate by April 1862.

By September 1869, it became imperative to build a larger firehouse, and a festival was held to raise money for the project. The new building would be on Wall Street, on property owned by the company. Once built, it was known as Huntington's first official firehouse. The two-story frame building, which measured 18' x 40', was constructed for $800. In 1899, with the acquisition of even more fire equipment, a two-story addition measuring 11' x 40' was built onto the original building. By this time, the fire department consisted of 92 members, and had one hand engine, one hook and ladder truck, one hose wagon, five hose carts, one chemical engine and 1,450 feet of hose.

The means for fighting fires remained very much the same, but there was a need to improve the alarm system. Just ten years before, a fire had destroyed the barn of Hewlett Scudder on Woolsey Avenue. Since it was necessary to rely on some observing citizen to ring the alarm bell located at the firehouse, when the alarm was finally rung, the firemen did not hear it and the barn burned to the ground. Greatly upset, Mr. Scudder donated twenty dollars to the department to start a Bell Tower Fund to purchase a new fire bell, and to construct a fire tower. The drive ended in January 1890, and a 730-pound bell was purchased. Later it was installed on a tower at the new firehouse on Wall Street. The system worked well for a while, until St. Patrick's installed a new church bell in 1907. The bell sounded exactly like the fire bell, which resulted in a number of false alarms. Arrange-

This building on Wall Street, now two stores, was Huntington's first firehouse

ments were soon made with St. Patrick's to have their bell rung in a different manner, to avoid confusion and unnecessary runs.

By 1906 the first telephone alarm system was introduced. Through the New York Telephone Company, all telephone fire alarms rang in Chief Sammis' store or home. By pushing a button, he rang a gong in the firehouse. Any person who heard it would then ring the fire alarm bell to summon the firemen. The Chief, too, would arrive to give the location of the fire. Also in that year, the voters of the district agreed to purchase a new gasoline pumping engine at a cost of $1,500. The engine was towed to all fires by a team of horses until 1910, when hand- and horse-drawn equipment disappeared altogether. The department now had a 25 H.P. Grabowsky Hose Wagon which could attain a top speed of thirty miles per hour.

The Wall Street Engine House soon became too small for the fire department, and was eventually sold for $4,500. There was a proposal to build a new firehouse on New Street, but it was defeated in 1910. By 1911, the proposition was finally passed for the Fire District to raise $15,000 for the construction of a modern, brick firehouse, two stories high. The 51' x 60' structure on Main Street was completed in 1912, and served Huntington Village for the next 46 years.

In January of 1922, the company got a new American LaFrance 750-gallon pumper, and in 1947 added a new 1000-gallon American LaFrance pumper. World War II saw many of the firemen flocking to the armed forces, which resulted in high school students taking over the job of fire fighting until the members returned.

Through the years the Huntington Fire Department experienced many changes and much progress. By 1957, traffic on Main Street had increased to the point where it was difficult for the volunteers to get to the equipment when the alarm sounded. A new location was once again needed, and the present-day Leverich Place site was purchased, with construction beginning in March 1958.

The Huntington Fire Department has remained there for the past thirty-eight years, and continues, through honor, courage and tradition, to protect and preserve both life and property in Huntington Village.

THE FRANCIS L. ROBBINS ESTATE

An imposing home on a hill near the Nassau-Suffolk border not only has an intriguing history but may even contain a ghost or two. The beautiful country home on West Mall Drive was once part of Long Island's Gold Coast estates. It is not clearly visible from the road, but once up the long and winding driveway, its history begins to unfold.

Built circa 1910 for attorney/horse enthusiast Francis L. Robbins, the attractive summer home was constructed in the locally popular early 20th century "Long Island farmhouse style." The house is virtually unaltered, although the property, which was once 109 acres, is now 2¼ acres. The rambling 2½ story six-bay gable-roofed house has a shed roofed entrance porch on square columns. It has massive end chimneys flanking saltbox-roofed wings, and a hip-roofed portico on the south. Owned by David Belding and his wife Lenore since 1985, the manor house has over fifteen rooms, including a center hall, remodeled kitchen, formal living room and dining room with French doors leading to a garden, a cherry paneled library, a wine cellar, servant's wing with three bedrooms, five fireplaces, three staircases, three family bedrooms and a master bedroom suite. An in-ground swimming pool and one-room cottage complete the property.

According to Dave Belding, an incredible ballroom and swimming pool room, built in 1928, were once connected to the main house. Three sets of eight-foot-high glass French doors led into the swimming pool room. It is said that Robbins had lavish parties during the summer in both the ballroom and swimming pool room. The architects were Delano and Aldrich, the prestigious New York City firm that designed the Otto Kahn Estate, Oheka Castle, in Cold Spring Harbor.

Unfortunately, the ballroom and pool room were torn down in the early 1970's. All that is left is an outdoor swimming pool. Dave Belding has photos from the archives of Columbia University of the original estate with its two adjoining rooms. The house was empty for a while, and vandals got into the ballroom and pool room, destroying all the windows. Water caused extensive damage, and the cost of repairing the structures was astronomical, so they had to be removed.

Dave is saddened that he never got to see the great buildings that once existed on his property, since the study of old houses is his hobby.

Francis Robbins and his family continued to use the house as a summer home until the early to mid 1940's, when Robbins sold it to a Mr. Price. If one travels south on Plainview Road from Jericho Turnpike at the Nassau/Suffolk border, large stone pillars can be seen midway down on the left side. (These pillars today are in Nassau County although the house is in Suffolk.) This was the original entrance to the estate, and is known today as West Mall Drive.

The Francis Robbins estate

On the original acreage there were several homes dating from the 1800's. Robbins used the extra homes for his servants. Many of these homes remain, on Old Manetto Hill Road between Plainview Road and Round Swamp Road.

There is a story as to why Robbins sold his estate. It is said that he was in a battle with Robert Moses over the construction of the Northern State Parkway. On a 1939 map, Robbins' property was shown, as well as the proposed parkway. As soon as it crossed over Plainview Road, the parkway went no further. The map shows it running right through Robbins property, then ending. Robbins' son had a house on the estate, and the parkway would have divided it. While Robbins and Moses fought their land battle, that part of the property remained condemned. According to Dave Belding, Robbins finally got tired of fighting and decided to sell the property.

Another interesting fact about the house is its relationship to the original International Boundary line of the 1600's. Blue plaques appear on both Jericho Turnpike and Manetto Hill Road, each marking the International Boundary line separating the British and Dutch Empires. On a map, if you intersect those two lines, it runs right through the center of the house. The house and the property actually straddle the border of the two empires that existed so very long ago.

Little is known about the Price family, who purchased the 109-acre estate from Robbins in the 1940's. However, Mr. Price began dividing the acreage before he sold it to Arthur Ludwig in the early 1970's. It was about this time that the ballroom was demolished. Arthur Ludwig died shortly thereafter, and his wife Trudy sold the 2¼ acre property to Dave Belding in 1985. The Beldings did not move in until 1986, however.

During an interview, Mr. Belding related a bizarre situation that occurred when he purchased the house. He and his wife Lenore fell in love with the beautiful country home the moment they stepped into the entrance foyer. They knew this was the house of their dreams, but unfortunately they still had to sell their old house. They didn't want to let go of such a find, so they purchased the house and were then burdened with two homes. The real estate brokers called the Beldings two days after the closing with a proposition for them. If the Beldings held off selling their first house for seven months, the new house could be rented out. It happened that the U.S. Government was interested in renting it. The house first was used by Republic Fairchild, the aircraft company; later the government put seventeen men from the People's Republic of China into the house. For a certain amount of money a month, the government would keep the Chinese there, and when they were through they were to return the house to the Beldings.

This certainly was not an ordinary situation. The Chinese technicians were put there to work on a surveillance system to guard the

Russian and Chinese border. The men were here from Communist China as invited guests. There were always Secret Service men and CIA around the house; after two months the neighbors got suspicious and lodged a complaint with the Town of Huntington.

As Dave Belding explained, "The neighbors didn't know what was going on. You can't see the house from the street, but every day they'd see seventeen men coming down the driveway to take a walk around the block. The Town had written a letter to me stating I had to get the men out of there. I in turn sent the letter to the Chinese men and they forwarded it to the State Department. The State Department told the Town of Huntington that if they insulted these people in any way it could cause an international incident. Nothing was said after that, and they continued to live there for another five months."

The Chinese eventually left, and the Beldings moved into the house. Dave, who loves history, made some interesting finds. He had always been drawn to Long Island's Gold Coast mansions, especially the Pembroke Mansion in Glen Cove, which was razed in 1968. Dave was familiar with a photo of Pembroke being torn down that appeared in the book by Monica Randall called *The Mansions of Long Island's Gold Coast*. He was amazed to discover that the bulldozer in the photo belonged to Norman Ludwig, son of Arthur Ludwig, the previous owner of his house. Norman Ludwig owned the company that tore Pembroke down. He later found out that Norman took marble from Pembroke and used it in the dining room of his father's house, as well as a sink which was used in the powder room off the library. Both of these mementos of Pembroke are still in Belding's house, as well as a cement baluster given to him by a former caretaker at Pembroke.

There were other intriguing things found by the Beldings. Voids in some of the walls lead nowhere, and there are dead spaces next to the fireplaces and behind built-in drawers. These things remain a mystery, but something even stranger was found in the little cottage which Dave uses for storage. It was known that an old surplus army generator was housed in the cottage, supplying back-up electricity to the main house during a time before Lilco's existence. One day Dave's son was in the cottage and found a metal canister which contained a manual for the generator. In big bold letters the manual said, "UPON

DISCOVERY OF THE ENEMY, MAKE SURE YOU DESTROY THE GENERA-
TOR." It went on to give ways of destroying it by using dynamite, gre-
nades, or burying it. A very odd find indeed.

There is another mystery that surrounds the house. Are there
ghosts in the old Robbins home? Dave and his family don't believe in
ghosts, but they do say they can't explain some of the things that have
gone on, nor the sense of uneasiness they sometimes feel in a particular area of the house. Not long after they moved in, they had a housekeeper living with them who stayed in the servant's wing. After several
weeks, she came to Dave Belding and said she saw two ghostly children playing in her room. They seemed quite happy and unthreat-
ening, but it
disturbed her
nonetheless.
She also de-
scribed a very
angry old man
whom she en-
countered in
the library one
evening. She
said he was
very tall and
was wearing
clothes from
the turn of the

Bedroom in the servants' wing, said to be haunted

century, and that he frightened her. Dave, not believing in ghosts, dismissed her story, wondering if she was crazy. The two incidents must
have scared her enough, though, because she quit the next day.

Another housekeeper was hired, and to Dave's amazement, described the same thing—the children in the bedroom and the nasty
old man in the library. Neither housekeeper had ever been in contact
with the other, and soon afterward the new housekeeper quit as well.
Since that time there have been no other sightings. Dave's future son-
in-law lives in the old servant's quarters now, and has never seen or
experienced anything. If the apparitions did in fact appear, it is un-

known who the children could be. Why, too, is the old man so angry? Dave joked, "Maybe he's mad because the ballroom was demolished." None of the Beldings have seen these ghostly figures, but Dave's wife heard and saw a fleeting shadow shortly after they moved in.

"In a big old house it's easy to let your imagination run away with you," said Dave. "On one occasion we did have an unexplained incident. My wife was asleep in our bedroom and heard a loud banging or rumbling on the wall that woke her up. She went next door to the den, where I had fallen asleep on the couch. She said to me, 'Dave, why were you banging on the wall?' and I said I wasn't. I told her I had fallen asleep on the couch." Dave continued, "When she went back to the bedroom she saw a shadow go across the steps. We have three staircases in the house, and the staircase near the master bedroom goes down to the library. That's where she saw the shadow. She ran back into the den and told me, so I went down to check it out. I saw nothing, but as I entered the dining room, I heard repeated footsteps behind me. When I turned around there was no one there. But nothing has happened to us since."

If there are spirits in the house, they haven't been enough to chase the Beldings away, although they do admit to avoiding certain areas of the house at night. The servants' wing with its narrow hallways and creaky old wooden doors, as well as the library, are less frequently visited areas of the house, although no one can exactly say why. "I won't go down toward that end of the house at night [near the library] unless I have a light on," Dave said. "Your mind can play tricks with you. It's dark down there, and for some strange reason it's always been the spooky part of the house. Period."

There is no way of explaining these stories or feelings, but for the Beldings, their home is just that—a home. The mystery, the intrigue, the history and the beauty are all part of what attracted the Beldings to the Gold Coast estate in the first place. "It really is a wonderful place to live," Dave concluded.

THE COLYER HOUSE IN WEST HILLS

West Hills today is the wooded, residential and horse country of Huntington, located between Jericho Turnpike, Route 110, Old Country Road and Round Swamp Road. The name West Hills was given to the area by early settlers, at a time when Long Island was still known as the Island of Nassau. The name was inspired by the highlands which extended from the north side to the center of the island. According to the Honorable Henry C. Platt in his famous Centennial Address in Huntington on July 4, 1876, "To West Hills came men of sterling worth, high character, patriotism, and love of freedom — men who shared each other's joys and sorrows and who were truly neighbors in every sense of the word."

The Whitmans were one such family, with a long history in the West Hills area. Poet Walt Whitman's birthplace is just outside West Hills on Old Walt Whitman Road, and many other homes lived in or built by Walt's aunts, uncles and grandparents still exist in the area. The earliest Whitman recorded in West Hills dates to a town meeting held April 1, 1668, and mentions a Joseph Whitman. It stated:

"Also it was voated and agreed the same Daie that Joseph Whitman shall take up ten or twelve acars of land on the west sid of the south path on the hether side of Samuell Ketchams hollow, it being toward his secon division."

There were so many Whitmans living in West Hills, the area eventually became known also as "Whitmanland."

Born in 1749, Jesse W. Whitman was a great-grandchild of Joseph Whitman, and was the grandfather of Walt Whitman. Jesse owned a considerable amount of land in West Hills, which he used as a farm. Before his death in 1803, Jesse Whitman had a deed drawn up dividing the farm among his wife Hannah Brush Whitman, their three sons, Walter, Jesse and Tredwell, and their daughter Sarah Whitman Walters. The deed was proved on March 20, 1802 with cousin Charles Colyer, John Carll and son Jesse Whitman as executors. It read:

"To my loving wife the use of the dwelling house I now live in and garden; also household furniture, provisions in the house and grain in the barn or elsewhere... and that all the hay and fodder on the place be kept to support the stock until my youngest son (Tredwell) shall arrive at the age of 21, then to be equally divided among three sons. I also give daughter Sarah Walters the cow known by the name of Starcow. My further will is that all the land and buildings that shall remain with all of the residue of my estate of what nature soever, shall be estimated by my executors... to pay to my daughter Sarah Walters 8 pounds out of every hundred."

By 1836, the heirs of Jesse Whitman were involved in several real estate transactions which included further divisions of the estate. Tredwell Whitman sold 80 acres to a Richard Colyer, husband of Tredwell's niece Hannah (daughter of Sarah Whitman and John Walters). On the land was a house built by Walter Whitman, Sr. in 1819. The home soon became known as the Colyer House.

The Colyer House in West Hills

The 3-bay, 2½ story gable roofed shingled house has a wood frame and a side hall entrance with two interior chimneys in the west end. It sits on a stone foundation, has a one-story entrance porch on square columns and six-over-six windows. It is connected to a 3-bay, 1½ story wing with small windows located under the eaves, and an interior chimney in the east end. A slightly more contemporary two story wing is located on the far east end and is probably an addition. (Although historical records indicate the wing was added during renovations in 1958, further research shows a photo of the house taken by Francis T. P. Plimpton in 1935 with the wing already in existence.) A vertical board barn on a brick foundation is also located on the property, its date of construction unknown.

The design of the Colyer house is almost identical to that of Walt Whitman's Birthplace on Old Walt Whitman Road, also built by Walter Whitman, Sr. in the year 1819. The well preserved house has been the subject of numerous sketches and paintings by artists George Avery, Rudolph Ruzicka and Hobart Nichols.

By 1850, poet Walt Whitman visited the Colyer house, which was then being occupied by his aunt Sarah and her widowed daughter Hannah. He wrote:

"These three days, we have been on a visit (father and myself) to West Hills, the old native place. We went up in the Long Island Railroad, and so in the stage to Woodbury- then on foot along the turnpike and 'across lots' to Colyer's; I plumped in the kitchen door. Aunt S. (Sarah), father's sister, was standing there."

Sarah and Hannah continued to live there for several years. Not much is known about the other owners of the house until the turn of the century. However, records reveal that a C. Colyer owned the house in 1858, and a C. Collier in 1873.

By 1909, the wealthy Robert W. DeForest purchased several old properties in West Hills, totaling 1500 acres. The Colyer house was part of the purchase. He called the Colyer estate "Sweet Hollow Farm." The artist Rudolph Ruzicka was a friend of the DeForest family, who were patrons of the arts and associated with the Metropolitan Museum of Art. The DeForests greatly admired the interior decoration of the Colyer House, and it is said that it became the inspiration for the American Wing of the Museum.

It is believed the house was eventually sold to a Mrs. Nichols, who upgraded and remodeled much of it. Later, the man who invented the ejection seat for aircraft, Andre Planiol, purchased the house from Nichols. Planiol, who was a physicist, was involved in the original Fairchild Corporation, and used the house as a summer home. He died a bachelor, and left the house and property, which by then consisted of about eighteen acres, to a French couple by the name of Brillouin, from New York City.

Stepha Brillouin sold the house and the two middle sections of the property, which consisted of two-plus acres, to Cherrian and William Levin in 1962. The Levins are the current owners, and enjoy living in their own piece of Huntington's history. Carved in a beam above their attic door "R.C. 1819" appears, probably standing for Richard Colyer and the year the house was built. It is details like this that make older homes so intriguing. A house can tell a lot of tales, and trace a lot of history. The beautiful and historical Colyer house is one such home.

FARM LIFE IN RURAL HUNTINGTON

There is a place where flowers grow and birds sing, where children play in the hay, ride in a wagon, build a scarecrow and feed farm animals; there is a place where hard work, tradition and family is everything in life; there is a place where people know your name, where people re-spect the earth, and where they enjoy simple pleasures like a sunset. To go to this wonderful place is like stepping back in time to a different era. It has all been made possible by a man who appreciates the simple and beautiful things in life; that man is John Mohlenhoff, Jr.

Born March 1, 1933, John Mohlenhoff (also known as Jack), came to Huntington with his parents and brother when he was three years old. The family had always farmed, with the first Mohlenhoff coming to America from Germany in the early 1800's. John's own family had a vegetable farm in Queens County. Eventually Robert Moses built a parkway that cut through the middle of the Mohlenhoff farm, leaving the house and barns on one side of the road and the fields on the other. Without access to the fields, the Mohlenhoffs decided to pack up everything, including one greenhouse, and move to the lush farm-lands of Huntington.

Huntington was all farmland back in the 1930's, and as Queens and Nassau Counties developed, more and more farmers moved to the Town of Huntington. They settled in Melville, Greenlawn and many other places where the soil was rich. According to John, everything that farmers needed was here: good earth, support facilities, and access to fertilizer and tractor parts.

The Mohlenhoffs settled in the c.1908 farmhouse which still exists on West Rogues Path. They were fortunate in that theirs was one of the few homes that had electricity. Every day the Mohlenhoffs worked their twelve acres, taking care of livestock, growing vegetables, and later, flowers. John had a very special childhood growing up on the farm, despite the hard work and the long days.

"I liked everything about growing up on a farm, from the day I was able to get out and run around in the dirt. We were self-sufficient. There were no supermarkets, so you grew your own vegetables, you had your own chickens. When company was coming, Mom would say, 'Hey, Jack, go out and kill a chicken.' So when I was seven and eight years old, I'd go out, kill the chicken, clean it and cook it, and Grandma and Grandpa could have a chicken dinner."

John grew up with many animals, horses being his favorite. "We always raised animals," he said. "Chickens, ducks, geese, pigs, all to eat. We had horses—sometimes one, sometimes two—to cultivate the land. If we had one horse and our neighbor down the road had one horse and we needed a pair, we'd put the two together."

There was an abundance of wildlife in the fields and woods—deer, pheasant, quail, rabbits, fox, opossums and raccoons. As the area developed, the animals disappeared, but John reported that thanks to the County's Water Resource Recovery Program and the saving of the open land around Pulaski Road and West Rogues Path, much of the wildlife is returning.

There were seasons for everything on the farm. In preparation for winter, canning of vegetables would take place in the spring, summer and fall. John explained, "There were some fresh vegetable markets around, and there may have been a couple of what they called Royal

Scarlet stores where you could get canned goods, but if you didn't have any money, the best thing was to do your own canning. We had beans, carrots, and corn; we'd boil them up in mason jars outside on a big fire, and store them in the cellar for the winter."

Most farms had smokehouses, and the Mohlenhoffs' was no exception. "Every fall we'd kill three or four pigs," John told me. "Neighbors would get together, like my Dad and Frank Franklin and Bill Wicks, and they'd slaughter the pigs, each one helping the other. Then they'd make bologna, metwurst (a German bologna), and smoked hams."

John recalled a typical day on the farm during his childhood. "You got up early and you had to have all the livestock taken care of — chickens, pigs, horses, a cow — before you left for school. Eggs had to be gathered and water had to be put out for all the animals. Then you went to school. There were no buses, so everyone had to walk. We went to what was called Lincoln School, across from St. Hugh's Church in Huntington Station. We walked whether it was raining, sunny or snowing. There were maybe a dozen kids in a class, and there couldn't have been more than 100 kids in the whole school. When I got home from school, whatever chores I did in the morning I had to do again at night." He continued, "Sometimes the kids from the neighborhood would come and work a few hours a day after school, for some spending money so we could all go to the movies on the weekend. My Dad would say 'Could you weed these fifteen rows of carrots?' and he would give them a couple of bucks."

Although farm life was, and still is, a seven-day job, Sunday was the day the family got together. Aunts, uncles, grandmothers and grandfathers would come every week for Sunday dinner. According to John, most of his relatives were farmers who lived closer to the city, in places like Jamaica, Ozone Park and Elmhurst. These areas were all farmland then. Many members of his family either lost their farms during the Depression and were faced with hard times, or had just sold some real estate and were living modestly. The Mohlenhoffs always stuck together and helped one another out.

"Our relatives would come out here every Sunday afternoon, and we'd cook on a big old fireplace," John said. "Huntington was 'wilderness' to them, and they loved it. For years they came by horse. Since it was a long trip, the horses would arrive very hot and had to be blanketed in winter so they wouldn't get a chill. When the relatives finally got cars and started driving, they'd strap a trunk to the back containing blankets, and when they arrived they'd cover the top of the *car* to keep it warm! My brother and I would hide out, laughing."

Huntington definitely was considered the wilderness then. John explained that if you looked in any direction you saw very few houses. Most of the homes didn't even have electricity until the late 1930's. Oakwood Road was blacktop, but was a very small road, about one car wide. West Rogues Path, which went to Cold Spring Harbor, was a dirt road; every spring, sand would be sprinkled on the road, and a truck would come by and dribble tar over the sand. Jericho Turnpike was two cars wide, and was a cement road surrounded by farms. Most were very small because farmers in the '30s did not have the type of equipment, mainly bulldozers, to clear large parcels of land. A farmer in Huntington may have had ten acres, which was then divided into two to three acre sections. The land was cleared away with horse and wagon, and was pushed off to all sides. The excess dirt could not be carted away, so each parcel would be surrounded by what were called "hedgerows." After World War II, heavy equipment became available, and produce being grown in the area became profitable enough to warrant spending $20,000 to clear the land. Three five-acre pieces would then become one large fifteen-acre parcel.

Huntington Village was a quaint, sleepy little town. Main Street was mostly residential, with few stores and no parking lots. John Mohlenhoff attended high school at what is today the Town Hall. He recalled Huntington Station as being a "thriving little community" and remembered when the train, which was only a few cars long, would come in. He loved the sound the old steam engines made.

The Mohlenhoffs grew vegetables for themselves and the public, and raised chickens and other animals for their own use. People would come to buy the produce, or it would be shipped to other places through a distributor in Farmingdale. The distribution was limited to Long Island because there was no refrigeration for perishable goods.

With the advent of refrigerated freight cars, produce could be shipped from Long Island to the South, so the Mohlenhoffs began to produce more greenhouse goods and also started growing flowers. The greenhouse they originally brought from Queens was now one of three acres of greenhouses.

"Our best crop was flowers, since there weren't too many [farmers] doing it," said John. "I remember when a person could buy a bouquet for $1.00. What really put us in the retail flower business was when men and women were going off to World War II. They would come to see my mother before they left, and they'd give her a list of important dates: a mother's birthday, a wife's anniversary. Mom would then send the flowers on those dates, and after the war the people would come in and pay their bill. That's when our business really flourished. All these men and women who were then married and had children, would tell their children to come to Mohlenhoff's because that's the lady that sent Grandma flowers in 1941. My parents really weren't looking to get anything out of it, they just liked to do it."

John Mohlenhoff Jr. on his farm

Mohlenhoff's Florist/ Nursery Garden Center is still located on its original acreage on West Rogues Path. From a very small vegetable and flower farm, it has evolved into one of the nicest florist and garden centers on Long Island. John and his wife Marylou have been married for forty-two years, and John doesn't think twice about saying his wife "is the best thing that ever happened to me. We have two sons, two wonderful daughters-in-law and five fantastic grandchildren. Although we can be thick-headed at times," John said, "family is very important to us, and we like to be together."

His mother is now eighty-six years old and still lives in the original farmhouse. John and Marylou live next door in the house that was built for them when they got married, and one of their sons, Mike and his wife and family, live next door in the third house. The days and weeks may be long, but everyone works together. Both sons are following in their father's and grandfather's footsteps, and to this day, all the Mohlenhoffs not only work together, but still eat meals together on Sundays. They are all happy to share their knowledge, love of animals and the farm with interested customers, keeping the rich history of farming alive. To the people who visit there, it is like going back in time. It's fun, and there is so much to learn.

The Mohlenhoffs have lived through many joys and hardships: the Depression, the Hurricane of 1938, the war, the fruitful crops and their family life together. John Mohlenhoff concluded, "You have to love the outdoors. I like the little things. I like to watch the hawks and doves. I see the sun come up, I see it go down. You pull into the parking lot on any evening, and we have sunsets here as good as in Hawaii. I'm glad we had to struggle in the beginning. Our family appreciates what we have today. We work very hard and take tremendous risks, but it's a way of life we like. I wouldn't do a thing differently."

THE ESTATE OF GEORGE MCKESSON BROWN: COINDRE HALL

In the early 1900's, the north shore of Nassau and Suffolk Counties was home to some of the wealthiest people in the country. Magnificent homes and castles were built, where plush parties and extravagant entertaining would take place. Its residents enjoyed the beautiful beaches and waters of Long Island Sound, rode fine horses and even raced cars. No expense was spared. Everything was built on a grand scale. Homes were often modeled after European art and architecture. The estates which were built were quite affordable to the rich because there were no property taxes in those days. It wasn't until the Great Depression that many of Long Island's "Gold Coast" mansions eventually were abandoned. The magnificent home of George McKesson Brown, commonly known as Coindre Hall, was one.

Coindre Hall

George McKesson Brown was a member of the family that owned the McKesson Chemical Company, a Connecticut pharmaceutical firm. He came to Huntington in 1906 and purchased 135 acres on a hill overlooking Huntington Harbor, where he planned to build his mansion. He had traveled extensively in Europe, and he wanted his home to be modeled after an eighteenth-century French chateau he had seen in the Jura Mountains near Dijon, France. The province was called *Cote d'Or*, or Gold Coast. He also brought over from Europe many furnishings as well as nine unusual trees, each from a different country. The trees were planted at the front of the driveway.

Construction on the home began in 1910 and continued until 1912. Brown's architect was Clarence Luce of New York City. The three-story, French chateau style home has a hipped-roof with two conoidal towers on either side. There are elongated decorative chimneys, steeply pointed gables and Renaissance scrollwork. Although the rear of the building was altered to serve the needs of subsequent owners, the building retains its overall architectural integrity.

Originally, George and his wife Pearl planned to use the estate as a summer country home. By World War I, however, it had become their year-round residence. They called their estate West Neck Farm. It was quite modern for its day, equipped not only with central heating, but with forced-air ventilation, a central vacuum cleaner, underground utilities and a private telephone system. Buildings on the original acreage included a boathouse and private dock (still part of the estate), a gatehouse, which is now the Unitarian Universalist Fellowship Hall of Huntington (on Brown's Road), a superintendent's residence which today is the "Caretaker's Cottage" at Unitarian, a chicken coop, barn, ice house and pump house. The gatehouse included a carriage house that later became the garage, a stable and part of the servants' quarters, including dormitory space for the chauffeurs of guests.

The boathouse, overlooking Huntington Harbor

The ice house was located behind the boathouse, and contained ice that had been gathered from a small pond formed by an artesian spring, providing pure water. Every winter, Mr. Brown's men harvested the ice on the pond and stored it in the ice house for use in the summer. It was then trucked up, tons at a time, to an ice room in the mansion's cellar, where it was used to cool the ducted ventilating air.

The boathouse, modeled after the main house, is located at the far end of the house across sweeping lawns. It once housed a very large yacht, nautical equipment and trophies. Simple yet elegant gardens and manicured lawns filled the entire estate, and views of the property and the water were magnificent from most rooms in the mansion.

The interior has a grand front entrance foyer with a massive fireplace. Several rooms contain fireplaces that were used more for decoration than for heat. Vaulted ceilings, terra cotta tiled floors, French doors, courtyards, a piazza, the cloisters, and ornate chandeliers all enhance the Brown's beautiful home. One of its finest features is the grand staircase in the West Tower—a magnificent spiral staircase made of teakwood. At one time the first floor of the house had a sauna bath and a fifteen-foot indoor swimming pool called "The Plunge."

Mr. and Mrs. Brown enjoyed their home for many years. Mr. Brown, who was devoted to fire fighting and prevention, was Huntington's Fire Commissioner and even donated ambulances until the early 1930's. At that time Mr. Brown began to lose his fortune and was forced to break up the estate, another victim of the Great Depression. By 1938, he and Mrs. Brown had moved out of the mansion and into the superintendent's residence, then known as the Farmhouse. He approached the Town of Huntington to reduce the taxes on his estate, in the hope that he could afford to remain. However, the Town refused, and he had no choice but to sell his property. Brown sold thirty-three acres, which contained the mansion and the boathouse, to the Brothers of the Sacred Heart, a Catholic Teaching Order.

Brother Martinian, the Provincial Superior of the Brothers of the Sacred Heart, saw the possibility of converting the estate house into a boarding school for elementary school boys when it became available in 1939. He and Bishop Thomas E. Molloy had been looking for such a place in his diocese for years. Mr. Brown sold the 33 acres to the Brothers of the Sacred Heart for only $200, and they took possession of the property on October 26, 1939. The mansion now had to be converted to fulfill its new role as a boarding school, without sacrificing any of its distinctive characteristics.

In June of 1940, two wings were added to the building in order to provide a chapel, dining room, recreation room, study hall and dormitory for the school. Brother Martinian was close at hand to make sure every detail conformed to specifications, and even Mr. Brown was available to assist in the project. It was decided that the new school would be named after the founder of the Brothers of the Sacred Heart, Father Andre Coindre.

Coindre Hall received its first faculty of thirteen Brothers on August 15, 1940, with Brother Oswald as director and principal. The first months were difficult in the new location, and enrollment was low. By the end of the first year, however, the charter had been secured from the Board of Regents and enrollment had reached 38. Diplomas were awarded to the first two Coindre Hall graduates on June 25, 1941.

By the second session, enrollment rose to 78 students, and by the third session Coindre Hall reached its capacity enrollment of 120. The school maintained that enrollment until it closed in 1972, at which time the Brothers sold the property to Suffolk County. The old estate building was neglected until 1980, when it was cleaned up and leased to a second school known as Eagle Hill. During this time, Coindre Hall was placed on the New York State Register of Historic Places in 1985, and was dedicated to the Suffolk County Historic Trust in 1988. The Eagle Hill school remained until 1989, at which time the building was again left vacant.

For some time the ultimate fate of Coindre Hall was unknown, and the once-beautiful estate was defaced by vandals. An official committee, under the guidance of the Friends for Long Island's Heritage, was formed to protect the mansion and the remaining 33 acres, and to put the building to appropriate use. This new committee was called the Alliance for the Preservation of Coindre Hall, an all-volunteer organization that served as the catalyst in its rehabilitation. The group is still actively preserving the site today, and Coindre Hall is slowly becoming the magnificent estate it once was during the Gold Coast era. It is known as the Museum of Long Island's Gold Coast. Limited tours, interpretative programs, exhibits and performing arts events celebrating the estate and Long Island's heritage are given. It was also chosen as the site for the Annual Holiday Showplace and Marketplace, which benefits the Friends for Long Island's Heritage as well as Coindre Hall.

Coindre Hall is definitely a place to be visited and enjoyed, because the former George McKesson Brown Estate is a wonderful example of an era gone by. Coindre Hall was given Local Landmark status by the Town of Huntington in 1990.

THE HUNTINGTON REGIONAL OFFICE OF THE AMERICAN RED CROSS

High Street in Huntington is a short, busy road that many of us travel on to get to Woodbury Road or New York Avenue. At the top of a steep hill on the south side is a large, brown historic home, over 100 years old. Outside, the Red Cross symbol is posted.

Where did the Red Cross get started? When did it come to the United States and to Huntington? What services do they provide? All these questions and more can be answered if one enters the big old building which was once a residence, and is now the headquarters of Huntington's Red Cross.

Born in North Oxford, Massachusetts on Christmas Day 1821, Clara Barton was one of America's great women pioneers. She was a teacher at a time when all teachers were men, and she won the right to a desk job in an office of the federal government in Washington, DC, when women were required to take their work home. She was probably best known, however, for her devotion to serving others.

Her service began at the age of forty, soon after the outbreak of the Civil War. Clara Barton saw the need to help people in distress, and decided to volunteer her services for this mission. From that moment on, helping others became her lifelong goal, and she paved the way for other volunteer groups who wanted to support those in trouble.

In 1869, Clara Barton spent time in Europe, where she found an even wider field of service. Some friends living in Geneva, Switzerland told her about the Red Cross. Her interest piqued, Miss Barton read the famous book by Henry Dunant, founder of the Red Cross movement entitled *A Memory of Solferino*. The book, and the Red Cross movement, called for "international agreements for the protection of the sick and wounded during wartime without respect to nationality, and for the formation of voluntary national societies to give aid on a neutral basis."

The first treaty incorporating Dunant's idea had been drawn up in Geneva in 1864, and became known as the Geneva Treaty, the Red Cross Treaty, and the Geneva Convention. The idea for service came about one year before, when a meeting took place to discuss improving the care of the wounded on battlefields. The Red Cross emblem was also developed at this time. It had been recommended that volunteer medical personnel from all countries should wear an easily recognized sign. The symbol of a red cross on a white armlet was decided upon, and this symbol, referred to as the "Geneva cross," remains. The Red Cross quickly became a symbol of humanitarian protection.

Upon returning to the United States, Clara Barton was determined to have the Geneva Treaty signed in this country. She fought hard, despite the fact that the administration of President Hayes looked upon the treaty as a possible "entangling alliance," and refused to sign it. It wasn't until 1882 that her efforts paid off, with President Arthur signing the treaty and the Senate ratifying it. Even before the signing, Clara Barton and a group of supporters had formed the American Association of the Red Cross in 1881 as a District of Columbia corporation. By 1893, the organization was re-incorporated as The American National Red Cross. It was given its charters by Congress in 1900 and in 1905. The 1905 charter and its amendments provided the basis for today's American Red Cross. With Clara Barton in charge, the American Red Cross devoted itself largely to disaster relief for the first twenty years of its existence. The Red Cross flag was officially flown in this country for the first time in 1881, when Miss Barton was appealing for funds and clothing in Dansville, New York to aid victims of forest fires in Michigan.

In 1917 the Red Cross arrived in Huntington, with its office located on Stewart Avenue across from the old Town Hall. Throughout World War I, Huntington was alive with patriotism. Residents showed their support by rolling bandages, drying and canning foods, and holding war bond rallies. One group in particular worked under the banner of the Red Cross. On August 30, 1917, the North Suffolk County Chapter of the American Red Cross was officially chartered.

Throughout World War II, the women of this chapter worked together, as in the rest of America, rolling bandages. In "bandage-rolling sessions" the Red Cross would gather and sterilize cotton sheets. They were then torn into strips, rolled into bandages and shipped overseas, to be used by the Medical Corps to aid the wounded. They also continued to supply disaster relief to those in trouble, and they organized and ran Red Cross blood drives.

In 1956, the Huntington Red Cross moved from Stewart Avenue to larger headquarters at 90 High Street, where they are currently located. Not much is known about the beautiful building which, as mentioned, was once a home. No information could be found on who the residents were, but the two-story structure with basement and partially finished attic has served the Red Cross well.

The American Red Cross on High Street, Huntington

"There is a lot of charm to the building," said Janet Hanania, full-time Regional Administrator for the organization since 1981, and a volunteer for the Red Cross since 1976. She remarked that the built-in china cabinets on the first floor, and the secret passageways and cubby hole in the basement bring a feeling of warmth and some curiosity as to who once lived there. Janet Hanania, the only full-time employee, receives help from her part-time employee of several years, Hestella Houston-Powell, and hundreds of volunteers who are always more than welcome to lend a helping hand.

The Red Cross still performs much of the services it did when it first came to Huntington. Know as the Huntington Regional Office of the American Red Cross, it is under the umbrella of the Suffolk Chapter of the American Red Cross in Yapank, and the International Red Cross. The Huntington Regional Office, formerly known as the North Suffolk County Chapter, is the largest and busiest in Suffolk County. They are dedicated to providing relief for victims of disasters, and in the last two years have give aid at the fires in the East End, and to the families of the victims of the TWA Flight 800 crash.

The Huntington Regional Office also runs valuable programs including senior choice groups, and the annual Children's Holiday Party and toy drive, to benefit our community's underprivileged children. They are involved in helping veterans at the Northport VA Hospital, offer assistance to military families, give training in first aid, run blood drives and conduct free blood pressure screenings.

The overall success of the American Red Cross is largely due to the fact that it is a major force in international and national humanitarian service, while remaining a local, community based organization. For over eighty years, Huntington's Red Cross has had a high standing in the community. The organization is an equal-opportunity volunteer agency. No longer is it limited to women, as it was during the days of World War I and World War II. Men and women of all ages have taken part in offering their services throughout the years.

If you visit the headquarters of the Huntington Regional Office of the Red Cross on High Street, perhaps to become a volunteer, note the American Red Cross memorabilia, which shows its service dating back to 1917. Posters found in the old attic show children, times of war, and times of service where the Red Cross was readily available. Proclamations for their outstanding work also hang in the rooms, with the oldest being the proclamation of the organization of the North Suffolk County Chapter of the Red Cross, on August 30, 1917. It is signed by President Woodrow Wilson.

Sometimes it's not the house, building or place that tells a story, but rather what occurs inside that can make history come alive.

ONE OF HUNTINGTON'S FIRST FAMILIES: THE SAMMISES

The name Sammis is familiar to most people in Huntington—in real estate and in insurance, in town politics, displayed on buildings, and used as a village street name. It seems the Sammis family has been around forever. As a matter of fact, as far as the Town of Huntington is concerned, they have.

I received much of the information for this story from the Historical Society, but also had the privilege of interviewing two 10th-generation Sammises. In a room overlooking New York Avenue in the Byron T. Sammis Building, I sat amidst old maps and family trees, learning about family heritage, childhood dreams, and what Huntington was like long ago. The brother and sister duo who told me their interesting family history are Quentin Sammis and Vera Sammis Murphy.

The Sammis family can be traced back to the 1600's. It is unclear whether the ancestors were originally from Holland and then moved to England, but in any event, a John Sammis lived in Connecticut circa 1660. Born in 1648, John moved to Southold, Long Island shortly thereafter, and then on to Huntington where he "was admitted a Freeman of Connecticut in 1664."

Upon his arrival in Huntington in 1663, John Sammis settled in the wilderness area of West Neck. The Sammises were originally farmers, and like many other settlers making their homes in West Neck, John had a self-sufficient farm. He built his home from the timber in the nearby woods. He and his family lived among other famous Huntington settlers such as the Brush, Conklin, Crossman, Leffert and Titus families. As the town grew, these settlers, including the Sammises, became involved not only in town government, but in different occupations as well.

John Sammis remained in West Neck for thirty years, where he continued to farm and raise his family. John married twice, and had several children. Between June of 1680 and June of 1681, Town records indicate that John Sammis expanded from his "medow" and purchased additional land from Benjamin Jones, Sam Ketchum, Thomas Brush, John Bates and John Teed. His property, at this point, had nearly doubled in size, thus expanding his farm. In 1684, however, John sold a third of his property to a John Ingersol. The purchase of the original property in 1663, the additional purchase in 1680, and the sale of property in 1684, were the first Sammis real estate transactions recorded in Huntington. More than 300 years later, the Sammises continue to buy and sell properties through their real estate business. In 1688, the first Sammis held a government position, with John becoming a "Trustee of Huntington Town."

John Sammis, the progenitor of all the Huntington Sammises, died unexpectedly at the age of forty-four on January 18, 1693, the cause of death unknown. The Sammis family continued to grow, however, and by 1880 almost every other house in West Neck was lived in by a Sammis. Although they continued to farm for several years, the Sammises branched off into new fields by the turn of the century. Huntington records show that the Sammises have been involved in grist mill ownership, boat building, brick making, banking, law, firefighting, insurance, owning and running stores (one being the old O.S. Sammis Store on Main Street where dry goods were sold) and dozens of other occupations that played a role in Huntington's development.

The Sammises have always been active members of the Presbyterian Church, and have served as Vestryman, Steward, Deacon, Trustee and Elder. In local government, positions held by Sammises have included Committeeman, Commissioner, Trustee of the Town, Road Supervisor, Clerk, Tax Collector, Assessor, Welfare Agent, Overseer of the Poor, and others. The Sammises are also recorded in war records, fighting in the War of 1812 and in the Revolutionary War at the Battle of Long Island. Many of those who fought are buried in the Old Historic Cemetery in Huntington.

Getting back to the 20th century, I received a wealth of information from Quentin and Vera about what their life was like growing up, and about their parents, grandparents and great-grandparents.

Great-grandfather Rinaldo Sammis, like his ancestors, had a farm in West Neck. He also owned a considerable amount of undeveloped land in Northport, on the site of the present VA Hospital. The area was still considered wild at the time. Quentin related a story that was told to him when he was a boy, by his grandfather Gilbert Sammis.

"Gilbert's father [Rinaldo], who lived out in West Neck, made a deal with his sons regarding the property in Northport. He said, 'Any of you boys who marries a woman who's brave enough and feisty enough to live out there in Indian country, I'll give you that farm.' So my grandfather [Gilbert] married Mildred Robbins. She was feisty, but she was a good gal, and they went out and farmed that land."

Gilbert and his family lived there for some time. It was there that Quentin and Vera's father, Byron, was born. According to Quentin, by the time Byron was four years old, Gilbert had heard there was red dirt in New Jersey that could grow great potatoes. So he packed up his family, sold the farm and headed for Freehold, New Jersey, where he lived out the rest of his life. It is interesting to note that the street which runs alongside the VA Hospital property is called Rinaldo Drive, after the man who inspired his son to farm the land.

Vera then told me about how their parents met, and the unusual circumstances regarding their names. At a family function, young Byron met the woman he'd spend the rest of his life with, the woman who would ultimately bring him back to Huntington. Lillian was a wonderful girl who had been stricken with polio. As she recovered, their romance blossomed and they decided to get married. The only problem was that Lillian's name was Sammis! She was from the same line as Byron—that of John Sammis—but luckily there were generations upon generations between them. They were cousins so far removed that getting married would not be a problem, although it did take some research in the beginning to make sure.

Quentin and Vera agreed that they had had many difficulties as far as their mother's maiden name was concerned. When asked, and they responded "Sammis," people either thought they didn't hear the question or that they were joking. Quentin recalled the problems he had when he entered the service and had to reveal his mother's maiden name. "No one would believe me," he laughed.

Byron, who wasn't particularly interested in farming, decided he wanted to go into business. His father-in-law, Jacob Sammis, had sold off the farm he had in West Neck and began his own business in real estate. Jacob asked Byron if he'd be interested in working in the business with him, and Byron jumped at the offer. It was the early 1920's when the two began the Sammis business we know today.

The little office was located on the northeast corner of New York Avenue and Main Street, where Hirschfeld is now (above the Bombay Company). Jacob ran the real estate business, while Byron started up the insurance business. They did so well that before long they moved to larger quarters just down the road, on New York Avenue. The Byron T.

Vera Sammis Murphy, Scott Sammis and Quentin Sammis

Sammis Building is a symbol of the hard work and dedication of Jacob and Byron, so long ago. Over 70 years later, the business that began in one small office has more than fourteen locations in Nassau and Suffolk Counties, with the Byron T. Sammis building serving as its corporate headquarters. Quentin is busy running the real estate end of the business, while his son Scott, the eleventh generation of Sammises, manages the insurance business.

Quentin and Vera spoke highly of their father, who not only built up the business but became active in the town as well. Byron played a big role in the development of Huntington Hospital, and he was also very involved with the Chamber of Commerce. He served as President for both these organizations.

Byron bought a house on Carver Street, where Vera and Quentin grew up. The two have fond memories of the old house, which is now used for offices. Eventually, Byron purchased land and built a house on Cameron Drive, where he and Lillian lived for many years. That house is presently owned and lived in by Vera and her husband.

"I loved my room," said Vera, remembering the house on Carver Street. "Quentin and I were very close as children. I had scarlet fever as a young girl and was quarantined. Quentin had to stay at our grandparents' house until I was well. He would draw pictures for me, and come by and hold them up to the window for me to see." Quentin and Vera smiled at each other. "We did a lot of things as a family, and we had lots of reunions," she continued. "On July Fourth we'd have a big party, and my father was notorious for setting off those horrible cherry bombs," she laughed. "The holidays were a special time, taking long walks after Thanksgiving, celebrating Christmas and New Year's together. We lived a very family-oriented life, and my parents were quite social."

Quentin interjected, "I kept a diary as a child, 13 or 14 years old. Good thing, because I don't remember a lot of what I wrote about. I read it recently, and I wrote that I went ice skating in Heckscher Park. I do remember walking great distances, though. We walked everywhere, to school, church, to town. Hey Vera, do you remember making the igloo?" Vera nodded and smiled while Quentin continued. "We got a lot of snow back then; we used to measure it and I'd record it in my diary. I remember the good sleigh riding streets were Dewey Street and Sammis Street, which was then Sammis Avenue."

I asked what it was like to be a tenth-generation family, and having a street named after you. Vera said simply, "It never even crossed our minds. Until recently we hadn't given any thought to it."

As the years passed, Vera became an entrepreneur, traveled, went to school, married, had three boys, and spent fifteen years in Venezuela. Like her father, Vera eventually came back to Huntington, living with her husband Bill in the old family home. She's proud of her family's history and has been involved with the Ketewomoke Chapter of the NSDAR for twelve years, where she served as Past Regent. In the past, she also volunteered time at the Huntington Historical Society.

Quentin had been in the U.S. Navy from 1943 to 1947. He married Ellyn Wenger in 1951, and they have a son and two daughters. He continued with the Sammis Real Estate and Insurance business, and also got involved in town politics, becoming Town Supervisor in 1966-1967, and Town Councilman from 1988 to 1992. He and his present wife Marge live in Huntington, as does Ellyn Sammis.

Both Quentin and Vera have seven grandchildren, which marks the twelfth generation of Huntington Sammises. Lillian Sammis died in 1969 and Byron died in 1979, but they left behind wonderful family memories and the Sammis Family Tree.

Quentin and Vera spend a lot of time together now and recall the years they shared in Huntington. Although the town has changed a lot since their childhood, they have no plans to leave. "Quentin and I enjoy it here," Vera said, "but my father Byron lived for the Town of Huntington."

THE WHITMAN-ROME HOMESTEAD

Sitting on a fallen tombstone was the "good gray poet." The long-bearded man was writing a lament about his ancestors' burial place which he called "The Sterile Hill." It was July 29, 1881 when Walt Whitman wrote this piece, which was printed in *Specimen Days*.

I now write these lines seated on an old grave doubtless of a century since at least, on the burial hill of the Whitmans of many generations. Fifty or more graves are quite plainly traceable, and as many more decay'd out of all form—depress'd mounds, crumbled and broken stones, cover'd with moss—the gray and sterile hill, the clumps of chestnuts outside, the silence, just varied by the soughing of the wind. There is always the deepest eloquence of sermon or poem in any of these ancient graveyards of which Long Island has so many; so what must this one have been to me? My whole family history, with its succession of links, from the first generation down to date, told here— three centuries concentrated on this sterile acre.

The ancestral hill Whitman wrote about more than 100 years ago is part of what is today known as the historic Whitman-Rome homestead of West Hills. Many perhaps may have recognized the house on Chichester Road by the huge script-style L on the chimney; for years it was known as the Langhans residence. It was occupied by Huntington's most famous Town Historian, Rufus B. Langhans, who until his death in November 1994 lived in this charming home, with the ancestors of the famous poet buried right in his own backyard.

The Whitman-Rome House

As mentioned before, the area of West Hills was often referred to as Whitmanland because of the great number of Whitmans who built homes and lived there for many years. The area was originally part of a 500-acre farm owned by Nehemiah Whitman, who was the great-great-grandfather of Walt Whitman. The present residence was built circa 1705, and research indicates it may have been built by Nathaniel Whitman. It is believed an earlier Whitman house stood on the site and was built circa 1660, but was destroyed by fire.

A barn and an apple orchard also existed at that time, across the road in front of the house. On a hill in the back of the house is the cemetery. All that was left of the 1660 home after it burned was the stone foundation on which the new house was built.

The 1705 five-bay, 2½ story gable roofed house has two interior end chimneys, a central hall entrance, six-over-six windows and a horizontal board fence. The timbers used to build the house were cut in the woods of the farm. Many renovations were made by various owners. New windows were installed during the 19th century; in 1937 the roof was raised to make two full stories, which provided four large bedrooms; and the front of the house was replaced in 1946.

The first owner, Nathaniel Whitman, willed the property to his son Nathaniel, who in turn willed it to his son, Nathaniel Whitman, Jr. It was then deeded to a Daniel Whitman, who may have been Nathaniel Jr's. brother. He was the last Whitman to own the property, because in 1821 he lost it for failure to pay a $1400 mortgage.

Walt Whitman never lived in the house, but his grandfather Jesse was born there on January 29, 1749. The house and adjoining property obviously were lived in or visited by many of Walt Whitman's ancestors, thus giving it significant value to the poet later in his life.

Samuel Haviland became the owner, but he had the property for only a year; it was purchased by George Rome on June 5, 1822. Rome sold the land across the street to the De Forest family, retaining the house and six acres for himself. The land he sold to the De Forests contained an old landmark once known as "The Spout." During the days of the horse and buggy, it was a popular public watering place. A spring ran through the area that supplied water for this purpose, and also provided water to local farms. Farmers would come by wagon to "The Spout," fill barrels with water and take them back to their farms.

The Rome family lived in the house for several years, with May Gelston being the last Rome descendant to own it. Annie Rome Gelston, granddaughter of George Rome, willed it to her daughter May Gelston of Brooklyn, who lived there until 1940.

On September 5, 1940, the house and now two remaining acres was sold to Mr. and Mrs. Otto H. Langhans. With their deep appreciation of history, the Langhans retained much of the old charm of the Whitman-Rome house. In fact, Mrs. Langhans was a former president of the Huntington Historical Society. Very much concerned with horticulture, the Langhans beautifully maintained the grounds as well. Upon his parents' death, Rufus B. Langhans, who had spent most of his life in the house, became its new owner.

Rufus B. Langhans was known best for his tenure as Huntington Town Historian, taking an active role in preserving our Town's history, and publishing over 30 volumes of Huntington's documentary heritage.

In back of the house is a path leading up the hill to the burial grounds of the Whitman and Rome families. Others families are also represented, including members of the Chichester, Pine, Baylis, Wood and Rogers families. Unfortunately, many of the old gravestones are unreadable. About 80 gravesites exist on the property, with the oldest decipherable one dated 1731. It is also believed that slaves are buried there, because there are plain, rounded stones unlike the others. Since the Whitmans had slaves in the early days, these stones probably mark their graves. Walt Whitman and his immediate family were not buried there; he and other family members were buried in a tomb that the poet had had erected in Harleigh Cemetery in Camden, New Jersey.

The Whitman-Rome Homestead retains its old charm, and like other Whitman homes in the area, is a reminder of this well-known family's past.

GREENLAWN

A LITTLE COTTAGE WITH A BIG HISTORY

On a quiet residential street in Greenlawn a little cottage sits. It looks as if it has been taken from some other time period and placed there. Literally speaking, it has. It is the charming home of Laura and Robert Dunne, who purchased the structure in 1989. "The Little Cottage," as it is known, is located on Arbutus Road, and has survived not only the American Revolution but a move from Northport as well.

The five-bay, 1½ story gable-roofed house was said to have been built in the late 1700's by Morris Bartow, who fought under General George Washington. The Bartows had several children, all of whom were born in the house. As the family continued to grow, the need for more space became inevitable and the Bartows built a larger home down the road. From then on they referred to their first house as "The Little Cottage." The name has been carried down through the years. The cottage was originally situated on Laurel Hill Road in Northport at the time the Bartow family occupied it, and was eventually moved to Greenlawn by the Rode family in 1945.

Features of the house today include a one-story shed-roofed entrance porch over three central bays, a one-story, shed-roofed wing on the north, six-over-six windows, and two "lay on your belly windows" of hand-blown glass. They are 1½ feet above the second floor, and are 18 inches high and 30 inches long. They were so named because of their proximity to the floor.

During the time of the Revolutionary War, it is said the cottage was used as a hideout for American soldiers making raids against the British; the patriots were concealed in a secret room in the cellar. A double stone partition was discovered in the house when it was being removed from its original foundation in 1945. Supposedly, this secret room was also used for distilling gin during Prohibition, and a rumor even suggests that it was once a house of ill repute.

In the mid-nineteenth century, the house, which was part of a farm, was sold to a William Woodhull Brush, although some sources list Harold Brush as owner and occupant. At any rate, it was in fact a Brush who purchased the house around 1844, and it is believed he lived there until his death in 1896. During the years the Brush family occupied the house, a lean-to kitchen was added on one end, and a 1787 coin was concealed in one of the beams. The coin was discovered when the house was being restored, and remains in the old beam today.

The Little Cottage on Arbutus Road

There were several owners after 1896, and eventually farmhands lived in the house and destroyed a good portion of it. They used some of the floor boards and molding from the second floor, and burned them in a flueless fireplace, which started a small fire in the dining room. After the damage was done, the house was vacated and remained deserted for several years.

In 1945, Russell Rode, a U.S. Army Corps Engineer, was riding home on the train when he happened to notice the run-down little farmhouse. That same evening he took his wife and daughter to see the cottage, which was almost completely hidden from view by over-grown trees. It had been his and his wife's dream, according to daughter Suzanne M. Townsend Rode, to buy an old house and restore it. The dilapidated building was going to be torn down until Rode took an interest in it. After checking the structure of the house, Rode determined it had many possibilities, and purchased the house from Peter Baiko, despite the fact his relatives thought he was out of his mind for doing so.

Upon buying the cottage, Rode was forced to move it from the original property. It was relocated about a mile away in Greenlawn, and its condition greatly upset the neighbors, who immediately started a petition to have The Little Cottage removed. Mr. Rode was amused by this, and asked the neighbors if they could refrain from going through with the petition for six months. The neighbors agreed. When Mr. Rode's son was discharged from the army in 1946, he began helping his father in the long and time-consuming job of restoring the little piece of history. In order to keep the original bricks, the chimney had to be dismantled brick by brick, then taken by the carload to the new location. The bricks were valuable because they were hand baked, resembling a loaf of bread. The massive chimney is located in the center of the house and has openings on either side — one that opens into the living room, and one that opens into the dining room. The mantlepieces for both fireplaces were restored, although one had been badly charred by fire.

According to a report given in 1954 by Suzanne Rode, who now lives in Florida, the original chimney had been constructed with mortar, the precursor of cement. The lack of flues enabled the building, which contained shallow fireplaces, to retain heat that would normally have been wasted through the chimney.

The original chair rail paneling remains in the home today, and hand-hewn beams located in the living room, dining room, and kitchen were exposed to give height and support to the structure. The ten- to twelve-inch floor boards were sanded and refinished to reveal the grain in the wood as well as the old square nails. No ridge pole was used in building the roof; instead, roof rafters were made, and were pegged with wooden dowels. The shingles on the house were all reversed, reattached and repainted. It was a tedious job, but the result of the effort was remarkable. The Little Cottage became a source of pride, beauty and historic value in the new neighborhood.

Besides the 1787 coin, a hand-carved clothes pin, a paddle or butter churn, and two framed pieces of needlework were found in the house during restoration. The needlework contained the inscriptions "Home Sweet Home" and "Faith, Hope and Charity."

The Rodes lived in The Little Cottage for several years, but eventually sold it to a Mr. and Mrs. Dineen, who then sold it to Gerald Dalven in 1972. Mr. Dalven was a member and Secretary of the Greenlawn-Centerport Historical Association. He sold The Little Cottage in 1978 to Mr. and Mrs. William Van Leer, and the Van Leers sold it to the Harris family in 1986. It was the Harris family who sold the house to the Dunnes, its present owners, in 1989.

The Dunnes continue the tradition of lovingly maintaining and restoring the little structure, and have no plans to leave. Like many people who lived there before them, they have truly made The Little Cottage of Greenlawn their home, and have helped it to withstand the ravages of time.

NORTHPORT

THE OLD COLONIAL NORTHPORT CEMETERY

Think of me as you pass by. As you are now so once was I. This eerie inscription is an epitaph on a headstone in Northport's Old Colonial and Revolutionary Cemetery, located on a very high hill on the south side of Route 25A, just east of Stony Hollow Road. It is on this hill that many of our forefathers, who fought and died for our freedom, lie at rest. The saying on the epitaph is true. As alive as we are now, we too will die someday. What contributions will we have made?

Many people think of cemeteries as spooky, morbid places to visit. But historic cemeteries can actually tell us many things, and give us insight into the past. The people buried in these places have had an effect on our lives, and have shaped the world in which we live. Those buried in the Old Northport Cemetery are no exception.

Like the familiar Old Burying Ground in Huntington, also known as Fort Golgotha, the Northport cemetery has a rich Revolutionary War history, and contains graves of some well-known people. It dates back to 1759 and has 202 gravestones. The last burial took place there in 1921, and it is now a historic and protected cemetery.

Many of the people buried there are original settlers of Northport and their descendants. They came from Virginia, New England and even from the Bahamas, and were farmers, storekeepers, shipbuilders, oystermen, soldiers and homemakers. Each had their own story to tell. Ebenezer Bryant, who is buried there, was one such person.

In 1700, the land and newly formed village (today's Northport) was named Cow Harbor, because cows grazed in marshland that is now the harbor. It wasn't until 1837 that Northport was adopted as its official name. During the time it was called Cow Harbor, it was also popularly known as "Bryant's Landing."

87

Ebenezer Bryant's home stood close to the harbor, on the north side of what was called the valley, on a bank at the foot of the hills. In 1790, a path was laid out across the foot of his property. It began "at a red cedar bush on the edge of a bank a little south of Ebenezer Bryant's house, and was all the way to be three rods wide." (It is unknown exactly what type of rod was used for measuring in those days, but it was a specific measure.) The tiny village called this path "Bryant's Landing." Eventually the little road became known as the "cordwood road" which led to Bryant's Landing.

The Scudders are another famous name in the cemetery, and it was actually their property on which the cemetery is now located. They are most famous for their involvement in the Revolutionary War and the Battle of Long Island, but they played a role in the development of Northport as well. There are descendants of the Scudders living in the Huntington/Northport area today.

Scudder family gravesites in the Old Northport Cemetery, Route 25A

In the 18th and 19th centuries, home burial was the norm, and families would set aside some of their property for this purpose. Family, friends and workers would be buried in these private plots. In 1767 the

Scudders lived in a house overlooking Northport Harbor. The property ran from the harbor across what is today Route 25A. It was in back of this property, on a hill, that the burial plot existed. As the town developed and land was sold off, 25A was built and divided what once was the Scudder property. The little house on the harbor was torn down in 1968, but the cemetery remained.

Many Scudders are buried there, but probably the most famous is Lieutenant Henry Scudder, who was a soldier during the Revolutionary War. He was a member of Colonel Josiah Smith's Regiment (a group of Long Island militiamen who set their sights on the British occupation forces), and also a spy for George Washington, a member of the committee to form the New York State Constitution, a member of the New York State Assembly, and a member of the committee to form and adopt the Constitution of the United States of America. He also represented Suffolk County for several terms in the State legislature.

There are many stories about the Lieutenant's involvement in the Revolutionary War. On one occasion, while Henry Scudder was out of uniform, he infiltrated the enemy fort known as Fort Slonga (origin of the name Fort Salonga), and returned with a map of British positions. This led to an exciting victory for the Americans, who captured the fort and burned it down.

Scudder took part in the Battle of Long Island; he was taken prisoner, but later released by Colonel Upham. Another time, Henry hid behind a log spying, with the British cavalry only a few feet away. Later, the Scudder family was held prisoner in their own kitchen while the British occupied the rest of the house. The British let Henry's livestock loose and used his hay for their own horses. There are two conflicting stories about another occasion when the British forced their way into the Scudder home. According to one account, Henry was hiding in the chimney when the British arrived. With a rifle to her head, Mrs. Scudder refused to disclose the whereabouts of her husband to the British officer, Captain Coffin. Unaware that Scudder was hiding in the chimney, the officer backed up; Henry then jumped out and killed him. Another account states that Henry hid in the chimney until the officer was gone, and that a week later Henry and a party of rebels surrounded Widow Chichester's house at the "Cedars," where the British were living. Scudder then shot Captain Coffin as he was playing cards, and took sixteen prisoners. Henry Scudder was also one of the most active soldiers planning raids against the Tories.

When the war ended, he and his family settled back in their homestead, where they became involved in Northport's development and lived out the rest of their lives. Henry had also been a minister, and built and designed, with the help of Charles T. Sammis, the Presbyterian Church in Northport. This courageous man died on January 21, 1822, having contributed greatly to our Town's history.

Henry's grandson, Henry Joel Scudder, is buried nearby. He followed in his grandfather's footsteps and had a military career. He was the Captain of the 47th Regiment during the Civil War, and he was elected to Congress. At President Ulysses S. Grant's request, he gave a speech marking the 100th anniversary of Huntington and Glen Cove.

Other prominent figures buried in the old cemetery in Northport include Joshua Rogers, son of William Rogers who signed the original indenture purchasing Northport from the Matinecock Indians in 1656; Deacon Thomas Rogers, a well-known preacher in the area in the 1700's, and his son Stephen; and Israel Bunce of the famous Bunce family. Two of Henry Scudder's fellow militiamen and Revolutionary War soldiers, Nathaniel Udall and Stephen Higbee, were also buried on the hill. Higbee had enlisted as a Private in the First Regiment in Suffolk County under Colonel Josiah Smith, and also signed the Declaration against His Majesty's troops in Queens County. Udall signed the Association in Huntington on May 8, 1775, and served as a Private in the First Regiment of Suffolk County Minute Men under Captain John Wicks.

It is through these men and Huntington's founding fathers that we can gain understanding and appreciation for the place in which we live. The next time you are driving by the Old Northport Cemetery, stop in and take a look into the past. There is much there to discover.

THE FAMOUS JONES DRUG STORE

The year is 1901, and the Northport Trolley has just begun operation. As it travels down Main Street it passes the little store at 90 Main, built in the early 1860's. It was rented to various proprietors until 1893, when it became a seed store and a meeting place for elderly sea captains, who were often seen playing checkers by the old wood stove. Now it belongs to Louis H. Jones, who purchased the building and opened a prosperous establishment that he calls Jones Drug Store.

The young man of twenty-eight graduated from the Brooklyn College of Pharmacy in 1895. He then completed an internship in the famous Hazzard Pharmacy in Brooklyn, where he learned about the incompatibilities of certain drugs, and how to run a soda fountain. Then Jones worked as a drug clerk for Henry W. Bronson, Thomas H. Botham and later for a Mr. Burr, before opening his own store. Using only real fruit juices and the finest syrups and ice cream, Jones' sodas became famous for miles around. He was able to open a full luncheon service within his store.

Mr. Jones takes great pride in his drug store, which is always neat and clean. The shelves are lined with bottles of drugs and patent medicines from leading companies such as McKesson Robbins in New York City, E.R. Squibb and Co. of Brooklyn, Parke-Davis and Co., and the Upjohn Company. Jones has a typical first-class pharmacy and only carries drugs that these companies manufacture.

Prescriptions come in from three local medical doctors, Dr. John Heyen, Dr. H.H. Davidson and Dr. Donahue, all well known in town. Even Dr. Doty, the "horse doctor" is seen at Jones' store. In 1901, the outlying farms have a multitude of cattle, pigs, sheep and horses, and farmers often come in with a prescription from Dr. Doty. For this reason Louis Jones carries a full line of veterinary medicines and products.

On the other side of the store is the ladies perfume counter where an assortment of Salon Palmer's perfumes can be purchased. He even carries a few French lines, including DeLetrez and Roger & Gallet. Nearby are sacks of rice powder that the ladies can buy to flatter their complexions.

Candy is a popular item at Jones Drug Store. Of course, Jones sells the ever-popular wintergreen candy and horehound, but he also carries boxed chocolates by Huyle and by Wallace. It's eighty-five cents for a pound of boxed chocolates, but for ten or fifteen cents you can buy them loose, and pick out the ones you want from the heavy glass dishes inside the showcase. Mr. Jones puts them in a small paper sack, and they are often eaten before leaving the store.

In 1997, we can appreciate the simplicity of those days. However, we often forget how difficult it was without modern technology and medicines. If a person got sick it was often life-threatening. In an interview with Mr. Jones many years ago, he remembered when all babies were born at home. He also recalled the first appendectomy ever performed in Northport. Mrs. John Scott had been extremely ill at her home on Bayview Avenue. Dr. George Fowler was called, and came out from Brooklyn. He was one of the first doctors ever to perform an appendectomy. After removing Mrs. Scott's appendix, he brought it to Mr. Jones, who placed it in preservatives. Mrs. Scott lived several years after the operation, but until that time if a person had appendicitis it was always fatal.

Jones was married and had two daughters and two sons. One daughter, Thelma, died at the age of three from convulsions. Mr. Jones, much later in life, remarked about how different things are now because of new drugs, telephones, cars and hospitals.

He always worked long hours. He awoke at 6:00 every morning and opened the store; he stayed until 8:00 when his employee came in and he could go home for breakfast. Afterward, he would return to work and often be there as late as 11:00 p.m.

Many famous people came through the doors of Jones Drug Store. Charles A. Lindberg, William K. Vanderbilt, William Randolph Hearst, Booker T. Washington and Mayors James J. Walker and Fiorello H. LaGuardia, both residents of Northport, were among the celebrities seen.

Famous or ordinary, everyone liked Louis Jones. He was a wealth of information, and he could spend hours telling people what Northport was like at the turn of the century, when he and his mother would come to Northport to visit his aunt. Although born in Newburgh,

New York, Jones always called Northport his home town.

In 1907, Howard Henschel built a small attached building on the right of the Jones Drug Store for his insurance and real estate business. It remained until 1922, when Jones converted the then-vacant office into the town's premier soda fountain.

For forty-nine years, Jones ran his drug store. He was 79 years old when he retired, and handed the store over to one of his sons for a short period of time. Eventually, it was sold, but the Jones name remained. It moved across School Street in 1971, with the address now being 100 Main Street. The building which had housed the ori-

ginal drug store became Northport Hardware, and it has been that way ever since.

Louis H. Jones died at 92 on January 17, 1965. Besides being a druggist, he was always active in local merchant's associations, was formerly a member of the Northport Rotary and of the First Presbyterian Church, and a former trustee of the Genola Rural Cemetery in East Northport, where he is buried.

Jones Drug Store is still in Northport and has kept its reputation as the oldest and finest. As you enter the store, close your eyes for a moment and picture the young man behind the counter in the early 1900's, with the shelves of hand-bottled medicines, the fragrant French perfumes, the sweet sodas and malts, and just then you may even taste the cool freshness of wintergreen or the rich taste of a small piece of chocolate taken out of a little paper sack.

THE COLE-SEYMOUR HOUSE

In the early 1830's, a dirt road ran parallel to the harbor in Northport. At one time running through the property of Ebenezer Bryant, this little road had been known as the "cordwood road" or "Bryant's Landing," and was later named New Street. New Street was the beginning of Northport's Bayview Avenue as we know it today.

The narrow paved street called Bayview Avenue is beautifully enhanced by elaborate Victorian homes, many of which were built during Northport's shipbuilding era. One home in particular, the Cole-Seymour house, is an outstanding example of Victorian style architecture. Not only does its architecture give it a place in history, but the family that built and lived in this charming home have their own interesting history—a history that dates to the time when oystering in Northport was a prime business.

Henry T. Cole was born and raised in Salem, New Hampshire. In 1808, at the age of 21, he moved to New York and learned ship carpentry and building. For many years he lived in New York and practiced his trade, before moving to Darien, Connecticut in 1850. Henry T. Cole died in 1874 at the age of 66, leaving a son and a daughter.

His son, Dexter K. Cole, followed in his father's footsteps. Remaining in Connecticut, Dexter learned the ship carpenter's trade at a young age, and worked in Darien for many years. During the Civil War, he served as master carpenter aboard the steamboat *Cosmopolitan*, which was chartered by the government to transport troops between Charleston and Fernandina, Florida. After a year, he retired from the service and began building small sloops and steamers in Darien. After several years, he became involved in the oyster business. The last vessel Dexter Cole built was the largest steam oyster boat in the business, and was the one he employed for his own trade.

Oyster beds were first discovered in Northport Bay in 1848. Oystering soon became the village's leading industry. The Town of Huntington, however, passed a law stating that anyone wanting to harvest oysters in the Town waters had to be a resident of the area. One source indicates that Dexter Cole came to Northport in 1889, while another gives a date of 1891. In any event, he purchased a house and pier on

Bayview Avenue that was built as a home and oyster establishment by Edward Thompson, whom Cole engaged in the oyster business.

Built in 1885, the 2½ story five-bay home is the finest example of mansard roof Victorian architecture in the village. (Named after François Mansard, the mansard roof was originally a clever means of escaping property taxes. During the 17th century, French property taxes were assessed according to the number of stories a house had, except for the attic, which was exempt. The mansard style was an affordable way of adding a story of living space, tax-free. In the United States, it soon became a popular style of architecture). The unusual slate fish-scale shingles make this beautiful home even more striking. The house also has a 1½ story side extension, a projecting central portico with a double-door entrance, segmental arched dormers and exceptional Neo-Greco bracketed cornices.

The Cole-Seymour House on Bayview Avenue

After three years, Dexter purchased his partner Edward Thompson's share of the oyster business, and then sold the entire establishment to George H. Shafer & Co. in 1894. This company is believed to have started the Sealshipt Oyster System, which became the largest enterprise of its kind on the north shore of Long Island. Dexter Cole and his family remained in the house, however, and Cole continued to run the business for the new company as general manager of the Northport division until 1914. At that time, he retired at the age of 78 and devoted much of his time to a farm he owned in Kings Park.

Dexter Cole had been one of three "oyster barons" living along Bayview Avenue. At one time, he was the largest local grower of oysters in the area. He died in 1917 at the age of eighty-one.

By 1920, Captain James Seymour had married Dexter Cole's daughter, Annie Lee, and took occupancy of the twelve room house. He, too, was an oyster fisherman who commanded oyster steamers during the time when oysters were plentiful. About 1915, however, the oyster industry began to wind down. Pollution and a starfish invasion had killed most of the oysters in Northport Bay and in the Sound. The Seymour oyster pier became idle for a number of years. Captain Seymour decided to build a shipyard behind the house, and it was his son, Dexter Seymour, born November 18, 1890, who eventually put the old pier back into use. Boats were repaired, winterized and towed in this shipyard, and Dexter Seymour became Northport's new Harbor Master. This shipyard remains today—the last one in 150 years of Bayview Avenue shipyard history.

The Seymour Boat Shop had become a local landmark in Northport, and was owned by Dexter Seymour and his wife Carrie, who took over the business when Dexter's father James died. Dexter and Carrie continued to live in the old house where Dexter was raised. The home was filled with memories of Northport long ago. Old photographs of Dexter's grandfather, (his namesake and first owner of the house), hung on the walls, and featured many of his oyster boats, along with other Cole and Seymour historical photographs.

In 1977, members of the Northport Historical Society built a miniature replica of the Seymour house, which by this time was as famous in Northport as the shipyard. In 1986, this unique doll house became part of an exhibit at the Northport Historical Society Museum. The doll house may be viewed, by prior arrangement, at the Northport Museum. It is a wonderful evocation of the beautiful old house in which one of Northport's historically significant families lived.

Dexter Seymour died in Northport in 1979 at the age of eighty eight. The house is still referred to as the Seymour house, and a large sign marks the site. The Attwooll family purchased the house in 1984 and sold it to Margaret and Dave Weber in 1996. They are busy restoring it, while Dave's son, Dave, Jr., is managing the boatyard. Although there have been many changes in Northport through the years, the Cole-Seymour House and Boatyard have survived them all.

NORTHPORT'S SHIPBUILDING ERA REMEMBERED

Strolling past the ornate, pastel-painted houses on Bayview Avenue, or past the quaint shops, antique stores and ice cream parlors on Main Street, one can't help but wonder how this small seafaring village (once known as Cow Harbor) got all its charm. Like an open history book, it occupies a special niche in the Town of Huntington, with its harbor, its historic homes, its trolley tracks and diagonal-style parking. Northport is truly everyone's all-American town. What few realize, however, is that early shipbuilding was the most important historic development that put Northport on the map, and led to its bright future as a great place to live or to visit.

Shipbuilding on Long Island dates back to the colonial period, when canoe-type boats were hewn from trees cut in nearby woods. This led to the production of sailing vessels, that would serve not only as a means of transportation but also as a way to ship goods and produce, both nationally and internationally. With the revival of commerce after the War of 1812, shipbuilding boomed, with sloops, brigs, schooners, terns and yachts being built for American coastal trading and for foreign commerce.

During the first half of the 19th century, shipbuilding emerged as one of the nation's leading industries, with New York City, Boston and Philadelphia becoming some of its largest centers. This new and prosperous trade developed all along the North Atlantic seaboard, including the north shore of Suffolk County. Three important centers form–

ed: Setauket, Port Jefferson and Northport. Northport was in a good position to respond to the ever-changing needs and revitalization taking place in the country's shipbuilding industry.

Shipbuilding was primarily a craft industry, requiring little capital to start. The shipbuilder was a hard worker, skilled at his trade, who also needed good marketing abilities. The shipyard owner was usually in charge of 25 to 95 men, and was responsible for making sure the vessels were completed according to the contract specifications, or with the market in mind. Since the vessel would be stamped with his name, its seaworthiness and durability would ultimately determine his reputation and degree of success. Often the shipyard owner would even assist his men in the construction of the boat.

The most successful and widely-known Northport shipbuilder was Jesse Carll, a native of the Town of Huntington. It was his excellent craftsmanship that made his service sought after and gave his yard a national reputation. Once existing on Bayview Avenue, at the site of today's Northport's Memorial Park, Jesse Carll's shipyard is remembered by the huge anchor that rests there.

It was 1855 when he began his business with his brother David Carll, both of whom apprenticed as shipbuilders in Port Jefferson before starting their own yard in Northport. In that same year they built two sloop lighters, each weighing about 80 tons. In 1856, the two brothers built their first large vessel, a 495-ton bark with two full decks. The partnership of Jesse and David dissolved in 1865 when David opened his own yard in City Island. Jesse continued shipbuilding in Northport, and through the years 1865-1890 he became the leading shipbuilder in Northport, rated AAA by Dun and Bradstreet.

In 1867, Carll built the vessel he was most proud of, the schooner *Jesse Carll*, declared to be "the handsomest craft of her class sailing out of the New York area." The *Jesse Carll* was used in the Mediterranean fruit trade, and she was one of the fastest vessels around, making the trip from Gibraltar to Baltimore in 20 days. Other important vessels built by Carll were the *Moses Rogers*, built in 1864 for the Malaga route, trading everything from wheelbarrows to sewing machines with the West Indies, and returning with fruit; the *Allie R. Chester*, a 144-foot centerboard tern, built in 1883 of yellow pine, oak and chestnut;

and the *Mary A. Greenwood*, the largest vessel made by Carll, measuring 154 feet long, with a 33-foot beam and a 17.8-foot draft. It was built in 1885 with a 1,100 ton capacity. Unfortunately, after six years of service the *Allie R. Chester* was lost in a gale off Cape Hatteras, North Carolina in 1889. A portion of her bowsprit was reproduced, and can be seen at the Northport Historical Society Museum.

Jesse Carll died in 1902 at the age of 70. Local newspapers estimated Jesse's properties, estate and business to be worth $250,000 at the time of his death. This was a large amount of money in 1902. Carll's son, Jesse Carll, Jr., ran the shipyard for several more years, mainly doing repair and storage work.

Carll and his son weren't the only shipbuilders in Northport. Bunce and Baylis had a shipbuilding partnership, although it did not survive into the 1840's. From 1841 to 1883, Jesse Jarvis ran a business on Woodbine Avenue where he built thirty-five ships. On Bayview Avenue, Isaac Ketcham, Edwin Lefferts and N.R.White were building vessels. The Hartts were also a prominent shipbuilding family who built ships as early as 1841 and remained in operation into the 1880's.

By 1884, it was estimated that approximately 18,500 tons of shipping were built in the combined Northport yards, totaling 180 vessels. These vessels included 91 sloops, 58 schooners, 3 brigs, 3 barks, 8 steamers and others.

Unfortunately, by 1885 the great shipbuilding era came to a close. Although some yards continued on, their businesses were not as profitable as they had been during the prime shipbuilding years. There were several factors contributing to the decline in the trade. One was that even though Suffolk shipyard workers were paid low wages, economical labor costs could no longer offset the increasing costs of raw materials. Second, with the evolving technology, steam-driven vessels were faster and in the long run more economical and efficient than wooden ships. The skill of building wooden boats became a lost art, overcome by technology.

There are few traces of the old shipyards of Northport today, except for the Seymour Boat Shop, a local landmark for over fifty years, known as "the last of the Bayview Avenue shipbuilders." It was owned by Dexter and Carrie Seymour, and operated by their grandsons for many years, as told in the previous story. The Seymours became the only ones in Northport repairing boats.

Seymour's Boat Shop and Pier at Northport Harbor

Dave Weber, Jr., son of the present owners, continues to run what was Seymour's business, keeping alive the memory of the long history of Northport's shipbuilding era. So the next time you're strolling down Bayview Avenue, or through Northport Park, look out onto the water with its many pleasure boats, and remember the industry which once helped put this all-American town on the map.

OLD TIMES IN NORTHPORT:
THE MEMORIES OF MS. HENRIETTA VAN SICLEN

Often the best sources of history are people. Everyday people live their lives without realizing how much information they collect along the way. Eventually they become a source of "living history."

I was fortunate to have been introduced to one of Northport's oldest residents. The meeting was arranged by another of my favorite history sources, Mrs. Grace Taylor, whom I had the privilege of interviewing several years ago. Through keeping in touch with her I was able to spend time with her special friend for over 70 years, who indeed has a wealth of historic knowledge — Ms. Henrietta Van Siclen.

Born on January 18, 1908, Henrietta was the second daughter of Henry and Florence Van Siclen, of the famous Van Siclen family. Her father had owned over 100 acres of farmland in Brooklyn before coming to Northport. The Van Siclen farmers in New York date back to the early 1600's, and were quite prominent, being one of the largest growers around. Farming began to change in the late 1700's, and as Brooklyn grew into a city, Henry decided to stop farming commercially, and buy a seven acre plot for his own use in Northport. Like many other farmers in Brooklyn and Queens, he felt it was time to move out east into the country and start a new life.

He found a beautiful, rambling country home on a long dirt road off Main Street called Ocean Avenue. The property included a polo field and an apple orchard. The Van Siclens purchased the two-year-old home and property in 1906. By 1908, Henrietta was born in the house. Mr. Van Siclen cultivated the seven acres and grew food for his family, and with the help of only one employee, took care of the land as well as a horse, cow, chicken, two rabbits, a dog and a cat. Henrietta's grandparents lived with them for a few years until their deaths.

Henrietta's father soon took an interest in Northport's affairs, and became involved in the community. He was a prominent civic leader, bank director, and was on the Village Board. Henrietta's mother did volunteer work for the church, and was a member of a needlework guild. As far as Henrietta and her sister were concerned, neither was to work until their schooling was completed.

The Van Siclens were quite fortunate because their home had electricity, and they were one of the few families around to own a car. They had purchased it the year Henrietta was born. Depending on the occasion and how far they had to travel, the Van Siclens either took their car or the horse and buggy. Sometimes her family would drive over to Huntington Village.

"Huntington Village was 'The Big Town,'" Henrietta said, laughing. "I love to drive, and learned at an early age. There was no age limit and no licenses in those days."

Many things were different back then. The Long Island Lighting Company did not exist. Instead, power was supplied by the Northport Electric Light Company, which was incorporated in 1893. Located on Woodbine Avenue, it was the first company to provide electricity to any part of the Town of Huntington. When the trolley came to Northport in 1901, it received its power from this plant. The Northport Electric Light Company later merged with the Long Island Lighting Company, whose main generating plant remained on Woodbine. Today, LILCO has a power plant at the end of Ocean Avenue, which Henrietta refers to as "the cove."

As a child, Henrietta remembered having spent a lot of time there. "There were two lakes down at the cove, and as kids, that's where we always used to skate," she said. "The property was owned by three families, as I recall. They were fresh water lakes, and quite shallow. A big sandbar was between the lakes and the Sound. In the summer we'd cross the sandbar and go swimming in the Sound. We swam everywhere — at Asharoken Beach and Crab Meadow. Sometimes we'd swim as far as Vanderbilt's pier."

Swimming was a favorite pastime for most residents of Northport, and summer days were always spent at the beach. The Van Siclens, although they did not own a boat, belonged to the Northport Yacht Club on Woodbine Avenue, and to a country club at Crab Meadow where the golf club is now located. It was at the yacht club that Henrietta first met Grace Parthenia Dominge (Taylor), at the age of sixteen. The Dominge family were summer residents of Northport, and Henrietta and Grace soon became great friends, spending many a day swimming together.

As a child, Henrietta attended school on School Street, now called Fox Lane. Every day she and her sister would walk to school. There weren't many streets then, and most weren't paved. They'd walk from Ocean Avenue to Highland, to Bayview and then up to Main Street, where they would take short cuts to School Street. According to Henrietta, Main Street looked almost the same as it does now, except that today there are more stores. She remembered a small grocery store, two butchers, a needle and pin store, two banks, one being the Northport Trust Company, and of course Jones Drug Store.

Everybody knew everybody else, and Main Street was a friendly place. Henrietta told me, "If you saw someone you didn't know, you'd come home and say, 'Mother, I saw somebody strange on Main Street!'"

The farmhouse on Ocean Avenue where Henrietta Van Siclen grew up

The biggest change eventually took place on the waterfront. As Henrietta walked to school she would pass the Northport House, which was the local hotel. When Captain Charles Aaron Hunt (born in Northport in 1883) retired from sailing his schooners, he purchased the old hotel, located on the northwest corner of Bayview Avenue and

Main Street. It was a village landmark. Businessmen, vacationers and local travelers often stayed there, and records show that even the Vanderbilts and Rockefellers spent a night or two. Local shopkeepers and farmers would also stop at the hotel for a cool drink on a hot day, as they waited for the arrival of the steamer carrying goods from the city. Next to the hotel was a shipyard, and across the street on Bayview was the stable for the guests' horses and buggies. Henrietta remembers there being very few houses on Bayview Avenue then.

A Mrs. Hendrickson was the owner of the hotel when it went out of business in the late 1920's or early 1930's. It was demolished in 1937, and the land was taken by the town, which turned it into the beautiful village park we enjoy today.

One of Henrietta's scariest recollections of childhood was during the days of Prohibition and the infamous "bootlegging" which went on throughout the United States. Many Northport residents still refuse to talk about it today.

"It was wild during Prohibition," Henrietta recalled. "We kids were half scared to death! At night the bootleggers would drive their cars filled with liquor from Eaton's Neck down Ocean Avenue — there were no turn-offs, just a straight road — until they reached Main Street. We weren't allowed to go out of our yards at night. These bootleggers were not to be trusted!" She laughed. "For about four or five years there was an awful lot of drinking going on in Northport."

"There was a speakeasy and all that sort of thing," she went on. "One time some boys got a little fresh; they spotted bootleggers coming in down at the beach, and when the men saw them they put them aboard a barge in the harbor and locked them up overnight!"

"When Grace and I went swimming," she remembered, "Grace was always scared. Every once in a while liquor was found hidden deep in the water. It was like that all over Long Island. We heard a rumor that someone was murdered, on a boat or something. I don't know who it was, or if he involved in something, but we were afraid to go swimming—especially Grace. We thought a body might float ashore. Once a log came ashore, when Grace was about sixteen. She had just gotten her life-saving certificate, and the other kids said she had to go and rescue the 'body!' She immediately went home and tore the insignia off her bathing suit, so no one would know she was a lifesaver."

Today, Henrietta Van Siclen lives in a house on Maple Circle, which she and her mother purchased several years after her father's death in the early 1930's, when the Ocean Avenue house became too big for them. Henrietta's sister, who married, had moved away, and it was just her and her mother.

By 1960 her mother had died, and she lost her sister five years ago. She recalls the happy times she shared with them, and although she misses them, she says that she has "seen and experienced an awful lot of changes in my lifetime." Melancholy for a moment, Henrietta continued, "Everyone's in a hurry now. The pace was a lot slower when I was growing up, and people were a lot more friendly. I was born during World War I, lived through Prohibition, the Great Depression, World War II, the Korean and Vietnam Wars. That's a lot of changes."

Henrietta is happy in Northport, though. "I really love it," she said. "I like being near the water, I like the trees around me, I like each house still having some land around it." In the life of Henrietta Van Siclen, these are beautiful things. One can find her happily communing with nature, or perhaps recalling fond memories of bygone days with her friend Grace Taylor, over an afternoon cup of tea.

THE TWO SMITH FAMILY HOMES OF NORTHPORT

There are two wonderful but very different homes in Northport, once owned by one of the village's oldest families. These homes, although under different ownership now, are known by the names of two generations of Smiths who lived in them: the Henry Smith House and the John C. Smith House.

Henry Smith was born in 1798 and died in 1888. He was married to a woman named Eliza, who was born in 1813 and who died in 1887. They were farmers in Northport, owning land in the area known today as James Street and Ocean Avenue. Although the farm was divided over the years, the old farmhouse on Ocean Avenue still exists and is called the Henry Smith House. The Smiths lived in the house from 1858 to 1873.

The 2½ story, three-bay, side entrance hall gable-roofed house was built sometime during the 1700's. The builder and architect are unknown. A 1½ story gable-roofed wing was added to the west side of the home circa 1840. A one story flat roofed-wing is located on the east side. The house has interior end chimneys, and sits on a stone foundation.

The Henry Smith House

The Henry Smith House is one of Northport's few remaining unaltered early farmhouses. It has wide plank floors, low ceilings, and vertical board doors with hand-wrought handles. Other buildings on the property are a barn, shed and garage. A panoramic view of Northport Bay and Long Island Sound adds to the charm of the house. The view was the result of an extensive sand-mining operation conducted along the shore during this century. During the 1920's it was purchased by the Shotwell family, who owned it until 1979, at which time it was purchased by Bill Martin, its present owner.

Henry and Eliza Smith had a son, John, on February 29th in the leap year of 1832. John C. Smith grew up in Northport and lived in the old farmhouse until he married Sarah E. Foote of "North Port" on March 7, 1855. John and Sarah lived in a house on James Street, just west of where John grew up. During that same year, their first daughter Lottie was born. By 1858, Sadie, their second daughter was born, and the family soon outgrew the little house.

During the 1850's John Smith had developed carpentry and home-building skills, and by 1860 he purchased land "down the hill" and built his second home on Bayview Avenue.

The John C. Smith House on Bayview Avenue

The construction of the house was typical of the Civil War period. It was built with brownstone below ground and local bricks for the areas in view. It is a wood-framed house with notch fastened milled beams and low gable roofs. The floors are held together with square nails, and are made of tongue and groove spruce planks varying from 7½ inches to 9 inches in length, depending on their location in the house. The walls are lath and plaster, and the original interior doors and trim are hardwood. Some of these doors and trim contain hardware with patent dates of 1863 and 1864. The kitchen/dining room was designed in mahogany paneling, and was located next to a well which was at ground level. Although the original well house is gone, the circular bricks remain. A small room behind the kitchen was where Sarah Smith did the laundry, using rainwater piped in from a cistern in the backyard.

Other rooms on the first floor are two parlors, a sitting room, and some bedrooms. The second floor has a curved hall wall and several bedrooms. Heat was generated by two pot-bellied stoves. By the early 1900's, an indoor bathroom was built on the second floor, replacing the outhouse.

The exterior is in the "New Orleans style" or "Steamboat Gothic style." It was built with fifteen sets of shutters, each coded with carved Roman numerals. The house was very ornate for its day.

In 1869, John's wife Sarah died suddenly at the age of 31. Sometime later, John married Elizabeth Bunce, a widow, and they lived in the house with John's two daughters. John lived to the ripe old age of 91 in Northport. The day he died, May 16, 1921, it was written that "he was one of the oldest and most respected residents of this village."

Even after John's death, the beautiful Smith home remained in the family, totaling 80 years of ownership. It was sold in 1941 by Smith's oldest daughter Lottie Droge, then 86 years old, to Minnie Chapman, the mother of artist/muralist Paul Chapman. Her son took ownership of the house upon her death in 1957. On May 29, 1963, a fire broke out in the kitchen, and damaged that end of the house. Afterwards, the house was neglected until it was sold to Janet and Dick Simpson in July of 1967; they spent much time restoring the house.

It was sold in 1978 to Owen and Ellen Coleman, the present owners, who made various changes to the original house. Although Dick Simpson has not lived there for many years, he has a special place in his heart for the old house. Now retired, he is the Vice President and a Trustee for the Northport Historical Society, where he researches and gives lectures on the various homes on Bayview Avenue.

Throughout the years, the Henry Smith House and the John C. Smith House have stood as charming reminders of bygone days, and of one family's Northport heritage.

COMMACK

THE HORSE RACING BURRS OF COMMACK

As one travels East on Burr Road in Commack, a magnificent mansion, set back from the road, sits proudly behind perfectly manicured hedges. The beautiful three-story mansard roof home is a glorious example of the architecture of days gone by. What most people don't know, however, is that the house is historically significant for its association with the locally prominent Burr family, who were among the initial settlers of the Commack area and who became successful horse breeders and trainers in the mid-nineteenth century.

It was 1630 when Benjamin Burr set foot on American soil, having emigrated from Essex, England. He was one of the original settlers of Hartford, Connecticut. It was his grandson Joseph who became the first of the Burrs to settle in Huntington, in 1714. A tanner by trade, he had a tannery at "Mosquito Cove" (now Glen Cove), and moved to Hempstead Harbor about 1719, where he lived out the rest of his life. Joseph's son Isaac was born in 1736 and eventually settled in what was then called "Comac" or "Winne-Comack" meaning "Good Land." What we know as Commack today was once a small village in the southeastern part of the Town of Huntington. Isaac Burr married Mary Baldwin, daughter of Sylvanus Baldwin who was one of the largest landholders in Huntington. Isaac and Mary lived on a large farm of 166 acres that he had purchased when he first came to Commack. He was overseer of highways in 1771, 1773, 1775, 1788 and 1789, and was often chosen as executor of estates. He died in Commack in 1830, but his spirit and his name continued to live on in the area.

The Burr family became wealthy landholders and were very important and active members in the community. Probably the most famous was Isaac's grandson Smith Burr and his great grandson, and great-great grandson, Carll S. Burr and Carll S. Burr, Jr. The three were involved with horse racing trotters and breeding, and became known for the stable and track they had in Commack.

Smith Burr (1803-1887) owned and ran a hotel that was the center of the community's social activities, at the corner of Burr and Townline Roads. However, he was best known as a breeder and trainer of trotting horses. Burr made a record as "the pioneer breeder of light harness horses." He was among the first to see that a large business could be established in this field, and owned the old-time trotter *Rhode Island*, as well as the greatest trotting mare of her day, *Betsy Bounce*. Smith Burr was also the first to introduce a new sulky — a light two-wheeled cart that he purchased in New York and improved. He cut off the top, made several other alterations and adapted it to his own use. The new sulky weighedonly 300 pounds, and was a tremendous improvement in the development of trotting horse racing.

Perhaps the most famous of all race horses foaled at Smith Burr's stable was *Lady Suffolk*, "the greatest gray trotting mare who ever lived," and for whom the song "Old Gray Mare" was written. Foaled on the Burr farm in 1833, she had three owners until she was purchased in 1837 by Smith's neighbor, David Bryant, a livery man who needed another horse. He paid $112.50 for her. One day Mr. William T. Porter, editor of *Spirit of the Times* (a racing publication) went to Bryant's livery stable to hire a horse and buggy to make a tour of the area. Fortunately it was the gray mare that pulled the rig that day. The mare trotted so fast and so willingly that Porter pushed her to go even faster. He soon realized he had no ordinary livery stable hack. Upon returning to the stable he convinced Bryant to train the mare for racing.

On a freezing February day in 1838, *Lady Suffolk* set a record for a mile heat, and won an $11 purse. She pulled vehicles weighing one hundred pounds or more, and was the first horse to trot a mile in a single harness in 2:30 or better, her time being 2:29½. From that moment on she established records in sulky and saddle, and trotted and won more races than any other horse. She entered 162 races, won 89, placed second in 56 and failed to place only nine times. *Lady Suffolk* trotted her last race in 1854, only two years before her death, and ended an incredible career which brought her owner much fortune.

The "Old Gray Mare of Long Island" became the "toast of the trotting world" for a decade and a half. She was a direct descendent of the all-time great *Messenger*, a famous Arabian horse which was the progenitor of all trotters in this country. Today, *Messenger* lies buried in Glen Cove under a monument dedicated to him.

It was Smith Burr who owned the large mansion on Burr Road, which is architecturally significant as one of the largest, most distinguished examples of the Second Empire style of architecture. (Characteristics of a Second Empire house are a square, boxy shape and a mansard roof with dormers on the third floor. This style was initiated when mansard-roofed wings were added to the Louvre in Paris between 1852 and 1857. The reign of Napoleon III in France [1852-1870] was known as the Second Empire, and thus lent its name to the architectural style as well.)

The Burr Mansion on Burr Road, Commack

The Burr family purchased the home shortly after it was built, circa 1830. It was extensively remodeled and lived in by Smith's son Carll between 1881 and 1885, at which time the mansard roof, belvedere (or cupola), and other Second Empire style details were added. This remodeling process reflected the changes which occurred throughout the Town of Huntington in the mid-nineteenth century. The Burr Mansion was originally a typical three-bay, side-entrance plan settlement period building, with several barns and stables located on the estate. Although many of the barns have lost their architectural integrity, the property today does retain a late nineteenth century barn and a small early twentieth century tenant's cottage which reflect the property's continued historic agricultural use.

Born in 1831, Carll S. Burr shared his father's love of raising and training trotters and he became quite successful. After his marriage, and the purchase of a 350-acre horse farm which he named Indian Head, horse owners in the area encouraged him to open a public training school for the development of the trotting horse. He then built a one-half mile track on the south side of Burr Road, which extended almost to Jericho Turnpike. His school became well known and he trained horses owned by William K. Vanderbilt, August Belmont, J.P. Morgan and Ulysses S. Grant, among others. Mr. Burr was popular, and although he never ran for political office himself, he was a Republican presidential elector in the Electoral College for Presidents Harrison and Garfield. Around the turn of the century, the New York State Legislature passed an anti-betting law which Carll Burr opposed. Mr. Burr always handled his business in a straightforward manner, and he believed the prohibition would encourage lawbreaking and would bring about conditions that were worse than the current ones. It was because of this that he left politics altogether.

His son Carll S. Burr Jr. not only shared in his father's profitable business, but went into politics also. He was elected to the State Assembly from 1896 to 1898, and then to the State Senate from 1904 to 1906. He was also very active in the civic affairs of Huntington.

Carll Jr. married and had a house built on Burr Road, not far from his father's home. The house was convenient because it was close to his father's and to the stables. The "Bride's House," as it was called, is historically significant not only because of its association with the Burr family, but because it is an intact architectural example of a late nineteenth century picturesque eclectic dwelling in Commack. The residence incorporates details from many of the popular architectural styles of the Victorian period, including Shingle, Stick and Queen Anne. These eclectic details include a three-story tower reminiscent of the Queen Anne style, flaring eaves, Stick-style-inspired ornament and a decorative veranda from the Shingle style.

Trotting horses were definitely his love, and together with his father, he built Suffolk County's first and only one-mile trotting track, which was located where the Commack High School now stands. Every week a race was held there and it created much excitement, until 1916 when interest in trotting unfortunately declined. The tracks became unkempt with weeds, and was only used occasionally for amateur races. In 1937 a pari-mutual betting amendment was considered for the State Racing Law. If passed, the track would have had a chance of staying open. However, the amendment was defeated and any hope of a public racing track in Commack was over.

The Burr family, despite what seemed to be the end of an era, made their mark not only in the racing and horse world, but in the community of Commack as well. Many Burr descendants still reside in the community, where their family's history and accomplishments are looked on with great appreciation.

THE 1789 COMMACK METHODIST CHURCH

In bustling modern-day Commack, there exists a little white clapboard church with a steep roof and a four-posted front porch. A colonial cemetery stands near the edifice, which has served the Commack community for over 200 years. The Commack Methodist Church on Townline Road, is rich in history and represents a time of growing religious needs.

Built in 1789, it is the oldest Methodist Church on Long Island in which people still worship in the original building, and it is the third oldest in New York State.

The Methodist religion was first introduced in Commack in 1783, when a Methodist preacher delivered a sermon to the community. His name was John Phillips, and he served as a tailor for the British army in Huntington during the Revolutionary War. He was also stationed to preach in Cow Harbor (Northport), and when James Hubbs of Commack heard him speak, Phillips was invited to preach to the people of Commack. His speech in 1783 was the first Methodist sermon ever heard in Commack, and it made a lasting impression on the people, so much so that shortly thereafter a Methodist society was formed. At first, services were held in private homes, and Methodist ministers who had been appointed to the Long Island Circuit would travel to various locations to preach.

William Phoebus, Pastor of the Society, inspired and assisted the Commack congregation to finally build a church of their own. Land for the church was purchased from Van Hadah Robbins "for two pounds and five shillings." The excited members of the community then had a "cutting frolic" in which timber and wood was gathered for the building of their church. Everyone turned out for the raising, and supposedly such notables as James Hubbs and Nehemiah Brush played a major role in the building and maintaining of the little church. The house of worship was very plain, and built much like a Puritan meeting house. It had no heat, so worshippers brought foot stoves to services to keep their feet warm. The shingled walls were uncovered on the inside, but were finally plastered in 1828. In 1895 a steeple and bell were added. Preachers spoke from a high box pulpit, so worshippers on the main level could look up to them. The box pulpit was remodeled in 1835 and again in 1859. The last change took place in 1889 when the pulpit was finally lowered to its present position. It is interesting to note that until 1866, men and women entered the church through different doors, and men were seated to the left of the center aisle while women were seated to the right. Phoebus remained both Pastor and preacher, but circuit preachers continued to speak periodically at the church.

In 1822 a schism or split took place in the Methodist Church of Commack. Several Commack Methodists had broken away from the Church and joined a group of dissident Methodists under the leadership of William M. Stillwell. They formed their own congregation and gained control of another Methodist church in Centerport. Known as the Stillwellites, these new worshippers dismantled the Centerport church that was no longer being supported, and rebuilt it in Commack about a mile south of the Methodist Church, on the west side of Commack Road. The newly formed congregation worshipped there for some time, their doctrine being that of simplicity. Eventually, interest among the members declined, and the building housed first a Congregational and then a Presbyterian Church. Finally in 1919 it ceased being a house of worship at all, and was converted into a two-family home.

The Commack Methodists continued worshipping at the little church, and by 1921 electric lights and a big central floor heater was installed. It was also around this time that people started to drive to church rather than take horses and carriages. An old horse shed once existed on the property where people would tie up their horses during services. In December of 1933 a special service marking 150 years of the Methodist Society in Commack took place.

The historic Commack Methodist Church

In 1936, war clouds gathered in Europe and anti-war sentiment was strong in the area. Several forums on war and peace were held at the church, causing much controversy. After World War II ended, new people moved into the Commack community and the church congregation grew accordingly. This brought about a need for an enlarged Sunday school facility, so the Church members bought an adjoining house and property in 1955 and built a Religious Education building which opened in 1957-58. (Along with Sunday School, the building today houses the Pumpkin Patch Day Care Center.)

By 1963, with continued growth, there was a definite need for a new sanctuary. The little Commack church had a seating capacity of only 150. This too caused controversy among the group, but they really had no choice but to build a new church. In 1965 and 1966, fund drives took place to raise money for the project, and finally in 1968 the first cornerstone of the new church was laid. In 1969 the new sanctuary, with a seating capacity of 400, opened with a special ecumenical dedication; all churches in the town participated. The 1980's brought about a mortgage burning in '88 and a new organ in '89. The new sanctuary is known today as the Commack United Methodist Church, and houses both Korean Methodists and the area congregation.

The original church is still being used, and its rich history and beauty enjoyed, although only for special occasions such as weddings, baptisms, funerals and during Holy Week.

The adjoining cemetery was part of the church property until 1916, when the cemetery was incorporated as a public plot owner corporation. The present Commack Cemetery is an outgrowth of the colonial burying ground which is adjacent to the original Methodist chapel. It contains graves of fifteen Whitman family members including Nehemiah Whitman, (great-grandfather of Walt Whitman), who was reputed to be the most successful of all the Whitmans.

Mr. and Mrs. Henry Shea of Commack are two of the oldest members of the Commack Methodist Church, Mr. Shea becoming a member in 1921 and Mrs. Shea in 1951. Both have been involved with the cemetery as well, and were helpful in providing information on both the church and the cemetery for this story.

Mr. Shea has been on the Board of Trustees since 1944 and Mrs. Shea has been secretary since the mid-1950's. Their whole lives have been devoted to the care and organization of both the colonial and modern day cemetery, and it was Henry Shea who had compiled a list of the Whitmans buried there. They have been actively involved in all phases of the cemetery including business transactions, expansions, burial maintenance, fund-raisers, planning for interments, putting up tents, meeting with people and yes, even shoveling a grave plot — something Mr. and Mrs. Shea both did! Mr. Shea recalled the old days when graves were dug by hand with a shovel. "It would take five hours to dig a grave alone, double that in the winter if the ground was frozen," Mr. Shea told me.

Mrs. Shea added, "If the ground was frozen you'd have to use a pickaxe. We were thrilled when graves could be dug with jackhammers."

According to Henry Shea, the land next to the old colonial cemetery was owned by the Brush family. When a need to expand the cemetery arose in about 1840 or 1850, the land was surveyed into 24-foot square plots with necessary paths. Plots were then sold by the Brush family for twenty to forty dollars until 1916, when the cemetery was incorporated as a public plot corporation. It was sold by plot up to 1960, when it was then sold by single space.

It continued as a typical country cemetery until World War II, during which time it was sadly neglected until the Shea family became involved with its maintenance and operations in 1945.

The original Brush property was sold by 1941, at which time an additional piece of land was bought from Carll Burr on about six acres. This area is now being used, after being divided into special sections.

As the years went on, improvements were constantly being made at the Commack Cemetery. A 1970 drive for funds resulted in the building of a $25,000 modern service building which included an office, the Superintendent's apartment and three garages.

A number of famous people were interred in the cemetery, among them three New York State Assemblyman: Honorable Charles A. Floyd, member of the State Assembly, County Clerk of Suffolk County and Supervisor of the Town of Huntington, circa 1870; Smith Burr, father of Carll Burr, and famous horse breeder and owner of *Lady Suffolk*, the most noted trotter of her time; and Caleb Smith II, Smithtown Town Supervisor, Justice of the Peace and State Assemblyman.

Other notable people include Carll S. Burr, New York State Senator, circa 1905-1912, three service men of the British Army and Navy during World War I, Orlando Hubbs, US Senator from North Carolina and Richard W. Hawkins, Suffolk County Judge, circa 1940.

The cemetery today is a pretty place, with over four thousand graves available and sixteen hundred already occupied. There are thirty different varieties of trees on the grounds, including sixteen Japanese cherry trees. The park-like cemetery is non-sectarian and is open to the public. An interesting feature is located on the left side of the entrance at the extreme north point of the cemetery. In back of the telephone company circuit box, which is located in this area, is one of the original town survey monuments showing the location of the Huntington-Smithtown town line. It is a granite fieldstone which dates back 150 years or more.

When traveling through Commack, take the time to see both the Commack Methodist Church and the colonial/public cemetery next door, to step into a world that existed long ago. It is through our ancestors and the lives they led that much historical knowledge is gained.

EATON'S NECK

THE DELAMATER-BEVIN MANSION

The areas of Eaton's Neck and Asharoken are known for modern beachfront homes, winding, narrow country roads, sea birds that swim along the shore, and the Eaton's Neck Lighthouse. What is not generally known, however, is that several distinguished nineteenth and early twentieth century estates and mansions exist beyond the woods, offering spectacular views of the water beyond. These homes are important for their architectural and historical value, and for the families who built them and lived there.

One magnificent Second Empire style home in particular, located on the quiet, unpaved road called Bevin, has been beautifully restored. Built out of a family's love for Eaton's Neck, the DeLamater-Bevin Mansion is a wonderful example of a bygone era, in which a home was built, lived in, and passed on from one generation to the next.

It was a beautiful afternoon in 1856 when thirty-five-year-old New York City resident Cornelius Henry DeLamater, his wife Ruth and their six children took a boating excursion along Long Island's North Shore. Cornelius couldn't help but notice the bucolic land at Eaton's Neck, which was founded by Theophilus Eaton in 1646. Cornelius told the captain of the boat that he and his family wanted to go ashore and explore Eaton's Neck. Upon their arrival on land, the DeLamater family met William Beebe, who owned Walnut Neck off Duck Island Harbor. They were so impressed by what they saw that upon returning to the city Cornelius decided to purchase land on Eaton's Neck, and began to research deeds. His dream was to build a summer residence.

Six years later in 1862, the DeLamaters' dream came true when they purchased all of Walnut Neck in Eaton's Neck from Mr. Beebe. The old farmhouse on the property was torn down, but its foundation remained, on which the DeLamaters would build their own home.

Construction began on a three-story, twenty-two room French style, summer manor house, that the DeLamaters would call "Vermland."

Cornelius H. DeLamater ran a very successful business called the DeLamater Iron Works in New York. It was originally called the Phoenix Foundry; Cornelius' father had worked for the small company and got his son a job there at age sixteen. Four years later, Cornelius was so good at his trade that he and another worker Peter Hogg, took over the business, since its owner was moving to California. Under its new name, DeLamater Iron Works, the business thrived. Boilers, armor plates and gun turrets for the USS Monitor were made at the iron foundry. Cornelius became friends with a famous Swedish inventor he

worked with, John Ericsson, and named his estate after Mr. Ericsson's homeland, Vermland, which is part of Sweden.

DeLamater had his home built of the finest materials, brought by boat from New York City. The large mansard roofed structure, which he built to house his family, his

The DeLamater-Bevin Mansion at Asharoken

servants and visitors, had fourteen fireplaces, twelve-foot ceilings on the first floor and nine-foot ceilings on the second and third floors. It contained a main staircase to all three floors, as well as a spiral staircase in the rear of the house. The beautiful one-story porch on square columns became a favorite gathering place for the family. The De-Lamater house, "Vermland," was completed in 1864.

A 20-foot by 25-foot addition was built on the west side of the house in 1886. It was three stories high, and contained 10 more bedrooms for the DeLamater servants, expanding the house to 32 rooms.

DeLamater continued to buy land on Eaton's Neck, eventually acquiring everything north of number 325 Asharoken Avenue. The only areas not purchased by the DeLamaters were the ten-acre government-owned Eaton's Neck lighthouse and Coast Guard Station, the Gardiner graveyard at Cherry Lawn, the schoolhouse for Common School District #19, and the Jones Estate.

Year after year, the DeLamater family would leave the city and come out to Eaton's Neck from June to September. Even when the children were grown they kept coming back. Eventually all five daughters had summer homes on the Neck, although his only son, who never married, did not build there.

Laura, Cornelius and Ruth's oldest daughter, married Curt Ramshon in 1869, and they had a son named Oakley. Laura was widowed just four years after her marriage. Later, she changed Oakley's surname to DeLamater, married a man by the name of Leander Bevin, and had two children, Sydney and Victor. Upon her parents death, her father's in 1889 and her mother's in 1894, Laura inherited "Vermland" and lived in the house year round with her family until her death in 1920. Along with the house, Laura DeLamater Bevin acquired much of her parents' property, which included Walnut Neck and East Beach.

Some modern changes took place during the Bevins' ownership, including a water tower built in 1899. Pressurized water replaced the old cistern and hand pumps, and by 1900 the house had electricity. In 1901, Laura deeded thirty-seven acres of the estate to her son Oakley, and in 1909 the Bevins had several cottages built north of the house that were used for servants and guests. The residence once referred to as Vermland became known as the Bevin House.

When Laura DeLamater Bevin died in 1920, the property was divided equally between her two younger sons, Sydney and Victor, with the house belonging to Sydney. Sydney used it as a summer home because his primary residence was in New York. Between 1934 and 1946,

Sydney took a job in Toledo and rented out the mansion. In 1936, the servants' wing addition of ten rooms was removed, and the wood was used to build a cottage on Bevin Road East. The Bevin House was too big for Sydney to handle, and the extra rooms were no longer needed.

Of all the tenants who lived in the mansion, the most famous was Count Antoine de St. Exupéry, the French pilot and author. In the study of the Bevin House during the fall and winter of 1942-1943, Saint-Exupéry wrote the children's classic *The Little Prince*,

In 1946, Sydney Bevin retired and came back to the family home, where he lived year round with his wife Anne until his death in 1960. In 1954, Sydney and his brother Victor had sold off large parcels of the estate that became Kew Court and Bevin Road East. Sydney loved the old home so much, that not only did he die there, but his ashes were scattered on the front lawn overlooking Duck Island Cove.

Two years later, in 1962, Anne Bevin sold the remaining property that surrounded the house, for subdivision. In 1963 the house was put on the market, and it was sold a year later to the Froessel family. Unfortunately, under its new ownership the former DeLamater Bevin-Mansion fell into disrepair, and the Froessels sold it in 1978 for only $78,000. The overall structure of the once-magnificent home had deteriorated so rapidly that for some time it was in danger of being razed. The home's fate took a turn for the better in 1979, however, when it was purchased by Laurie and Niko Kefalidis, who painstakingly restored it to its former glory over a period of several years.

Today, the DeLamater-Bevin Mansion is one of the oldest extant dwellings in the Village of Asharoken's Eaton's Neck. It is significant for its fine Second Empire style architectural features, but is perhaps more famous for the generations of families who loved and appreciated not only the house, but the beauty and tranquillity of Eaton's Neck.

(More information on the DeLamater-Bevin families, and on Eaton's Neck and Asharoken, can be found in Edward Carr's book *Faded Laurels, The History of Eaton's Neck and Asharoken*, where much of the factual information for this story was obtained).

HALESITE

THE HISTORY OF BROWN BROTHERS POTTERY

The tradition of pottery-making in Huntington can be traced back as far as 1805, and lasted for one hundred years. When this wonderful and useful art began to wane, it signaled the end to an industry that will never be seen again. The Huntington pottery was the longest running pottery business on Long Island, and perhaps the most famous.

Early potters decided to come to Huntington for two reasons. First, rich clay deposits had been found along its shoreline, and secondly, its easy access to Long Island Sound provided a means by which pottery could be shipped by boat to various locations on Long Island, New York City and across the Sound to Connecticut.

The pottery industry in Huntington is said to have officially begun in the year 1805. The cover page of a deed was traced, stating the following: "Timothy William Deed, May 8, 1805, for the Pottery." Records indicate that four men named Wetmore, Fleet, Sammis and Scudder operated the newly formed pottery, which they called the Wetmore Company. The four men were not potters by trade, so they employed well-known potters from various other areas, the best known being John Betts Gregory from Norwalk, Connecticut. For reasons unknown, the pottery eventually came under the sole proprietorship of Moses Scudder, who sold the pottery a few months before his death in 1825 to Benjamin Keeler. Keeler purchased the three-quarter-acre property on which the pottery was located for $1,300. After making several improvements to the pottery, he sold it two years later, in 1827, for $3,100.

Matthew H. Gardiner and Henry Lewis were partners who purchased the Huntington pottery from Benjamin Keeler. Like the four men who had founded it, Gardiner and Lewis were not potters, and hired reputable men to produce the pottery. Gardiner left the firm in

1829, passing full ownership over to Lewis, who continued to run the pottery for the next twenty-seven years. Under the company name of Lewis and Gardiner, they were the first Huntington potters to stamp their work with the firm's name. Eventually the pottery was stamped "Lewis," "H. Lewis" and finally "Lewis and Lewis," when a J. R. Lewis appears in records. He may have been a brother or son of Henry Lewis. At any rate, the Lewises sold the pottery in 1854 to Isaac Scudder Ketcham and Francis S. Hoyt.

Ketcham had purchased his share of the pottery for his son-in-law, Frederick J. Caire, who had been employed under Lewis' ownership since the 1840's. Caire had been the pottery's manager under Ketcham and Hoyt, and he became a partner when Hoyt dropped out of the partnership with Ketcham in 1863. Stone and earthenware were successfully produced at the pottery in the forms of butter churns, crocks, pots and jugs. Most of the work produced by Caire was stamped "F. J. Caire, Huntington, L.I.."

During the Civil War, Caire was drafted into the Union army, and with no one left to run the pottery, Ketcham was forced to sell it. It was at this time, in 1863, that the subjects of this story came to Huntington and purchased the pottery. Known as the Brown Brothers, they would become the most famous owners of the business and operated it for the longest period of time. Their business was located at the same site as the previous pottery, on the west side of today's East Shore Road, east of Huntington Harbor and just north of Halesite Park.

The three brothers — George, Stephen and Thomas Brown — were from the Hudson River city of Poughkeepsie, which produced some of the best potters, and pottery, in the state. Included in this group of potters was Frederick Caire, and two of Caire's children eventually married members of the Brown family. Daughter Julia Caire married the son of pottery owner George Brown in 1875, and Lewis Caire married Stephen's eldest daughter Emily Brown in 1881, forming a sort of "potting clan."

The three Brown Brothers had been in business together for five years when in 1868 the partnership was dissolved, and only George and Thomas remained. Stephen came back as co-proprietor in 1873, perhaps because his brother Thomas had left Huntington between the years 1870-1880, with George running the business on his own. Stephen left the pottery again in 1879, but this time to establish his own pottery on the west side of New York Avenue, about a mile from the Brown Brothers Pottery. His new business lasted only a short time, because records indicate that in 1882 he moved to Tom's River, New Jersey, where he managed a seven-hundred-acre farm. Brother Thomas appeared once more in 1880, returning to the pottery and working as a potter only.

George Brown was now the sole owner and proprietor of Brown Brothers Pottery. A few years later, George's son, George W. Brown, entered the business. They worked together until 1898, when George retired and left the business to his son, who continued it until his own retirement.

The Brown family and their pottery were important parts of Huntington's past. Many of their pieces can be found throughout Huntington, and are of great value today. In addition to Brown Brothers pottery, two Brown homes still exist on East Shore Road in Halesite.

The first house is a three-bay, 2½ story gable roofed, side hall entrance, clapboard and shingled house. It has a 1½ story three-bay wing on the north side, a one-story porch on both sections, and a small one-story gable roofed wing to the far north. It was constructed circa 1865 for George Brown, who wanted to live close to his pottery works. Some structural evidence indicates the southern part of the house may have been built earlier than 1865, and that the Browns may have enlarged it. The house remains virtually unaltered, and is important for its association with Brown Brothers pottery.

The second Brown house was constructed by George Brown sometime between 1873 and 1880 for his son George W. Brown, when he entered his father's business. The 2½ story, gable-roofed clapboard house has a one-story copper-roofed porch on two sides. Interestingly enough, it appeared in an Edward Lange painting of the Brown Brothers pottery in 1880. George W. Brown lived there with his wife Julia Caire until 1915, when he conveyed the house to his youngest daughter, Carrie E. Brown, who lived there until her death in 1976. When she died, Carrie Brown left behind family records and papers, a Caire family Bible, Brown family pottery and potting tools.

The Carrie Brown House on East Shore Road

Brown Brothers continued producing pottery until newer, more modern ways were devised to preserve food. Canned food was available for purchase, and those willing to do home canning could use the new glass jars. These developments and the advances in refrigeration made pottery almost obsolete, with stoneware disappearing altogether.

The pottery finally closed in 1905, and over 100 years of an industry came to an end. The structures where the pottery was made were eventually torn down, the last one being destroyed in 1918. The site which had been occupied by a pottery until 1905 was built over to some extent, but occasionally remnants of pottery can still be found.

The Brown Brothers were so successful because they not only were expert craftsman in stoneware and earthenware, but the family stayed together as a commercial entity for almost 50 years. The Browns are significant in Huntington's history as well as that of New York State.

Though they are hard to come by, pieces of Brown Brothers pottery can still be purchased, mainly through antique dealers. What once may have cost a few dollars can be worth several hundred dollars today. To ensure authenticity, look for the following marks: "Brown &

Bros./Huntington L.I." (this being the oldest and most valuable), "Brown Brothers/Huntington L.I.," "Brown Brother ./ Huntington L.I. (there is no "s" but a space was left for one), and "S.C. Brown /Huntington L.I." which was from Stephen Brown's pottery on the west side of New York Avenue. Many of the pieces made at Stephen's pottery were quite unique; they were some of the finest around because stencils were often used, and many pieces had sayings or epitaphs on them.

Brown Brothers' pottery on display at the
Huntington Historical Society's Conklin House

Brown Brothers' pots, pitchers, jugs, vases, urns, dishes, teapots, butter churns and other pieces, are all works of art as well as fine collectible antiques. So take a look at what is lying around in your basement, or at a local yard sale. One never knows. You just may be lucky enough to find a wonderful piece of Huntington's pottery history.

(Further information on Brown Brothers Pottery can be found in *Useful Art: Long Island Pottery*, by Cynthia Arps Corbett for the Society for the Preservation of Long Island Antiquities.)

GROWING UP WITH THE KNUTSONS

Often I get ideas for stories in unusual ways. My husband and I are frequent customers at T.K.'s Galley, a restaurant in Halesite. We have often spoken with its owner, Torkel Knutson, known as "T.K.," about the Norwegian family he came from, a family of famous shipbuilders who worked both in Huntington and abroad. I decided to do some research on the Knutson family, and T.K. was happy to tell me about his family's history, and about his own life in Huntington.

I've often seen and admired a magnificent, rambling white house known as "East Point." It juts out into Huntington Harbor on three acres of land, and always has the American flag proudly flying. What I hadn't known was that the Knutson family lived in East Point for several years.

T.K. put me in touch with its present owner, Mrs. Gloria Nostrand. She too had a wealth of information, and some very unusual stories to tell. At this point that I decided to divide their stories into two sections, since each had its own importance. Mrs. Nostrand's account of East Point appears in the Huntington Bay section. But first let's take a trip down memory lane with Torkel Knutson.

Entering T.K.'s Galley is like taking a step back in time. The nautical theme and the simplicity of the decor brings you back to an era when everyone knew everyone else in town. It is still a place where families spend time together — the all-American, local gathering place. T.K. and I sat at a table, with dozens of old 8x10 black and white photographs hanging on a wall behind us. The photos, many of them T.K.'s and others that were given to him by customers, show scenes of Huntington: fishing boats, marinas, and of course, East Point. For two hours we discussed the Knutsons' heritage and their accomplishments. It all began in Norway, centuries ago.

I started with the two most common questions: First, what is the right way to pronounce "Knutson," and second, does everyone in the family have blond hair and blue eyes? T.K. laughed and told me that Norwegians do pronounce the K, and that of his parents' twelve children, six were redheads and six were blondes.

On a more serious note, we began talking about his grandfather, who was born into a Norwegian shipbuilding family in 1894. Given the birth name Torkel "Knudsen," he changed his name to "Thomas Knutson" when he came to America at the age of seventeen, by way of Ellis Island. He Americanized his name because he felt he would have a better chance at getting a job.

Familiar with boats and with shipbuilding, Thomas first worked in a small boat shop on the Harlem River. He spent many years living and working in the city, and eventually had a ship-yard of his own. He be-came the superinten-dent of the New York Yacht, Launch and En-gine Co. By 1934 he started the Central Ship Yards in Lawrence, Long Island, where he became quite successful.

In 1938, Thomas Knutson purchased the W.E. Abrams Shipyards in Halesite, which he found to be a wonderful opportunity. He moved his wife and children to Huntington, and lived with them above the

Torkel "T.K." Knutson at his restaurant

yards. The shipyards had been built circa 1924 for Walter E. Abrams, after he purchased the site once occupied by the old Edgewater Hotel. The area had been used for shipbuilding activities since the 1830's, with a lapse for the hotel use in the late 19th and early 20th centuries. The yards, still carrying the Knutson name today, are the last ship-building site in Huntington.

Thomas Knutson thrived at his trade, and had over five hundred employees. He brought more than half of them over from Norway. He soon was able to purchase a home on Bay Avenue, as well as in Norway, where the family frequently visited. The Norway house was owned by one of Thomas's grandmother's relatives.

Since his arrival in New York at seventeen, Thomas had built hundreds of boats. During World War II he built sub-chasers, rescue boats, landing barges and tug boats. He also built boats for the police force, and luxury boats, yachts, speedboats and skiffs for private purchasers. According to T.K., his grandfather was supposed to build a boat for President John F. Kennedy. At the time the President was shot, he was in the middle of designing the plans.

One of his children, Thomas, learned the family trade and worked with Thomas Sr. in the shipyards as he got older. Known throughout Huntington as Arthur, young Thomas eventually took over the ship-building business, and even became president of the New York Boat Builders Association for three terms.

It was at the Knutson Shipyards that T.K.'s parents first met. His mother's father was interested in purchasing a boat, and through the transactions, his parents eventually became acquainted. T.K.'s mother was originally from Brooklyn. Her family spent the summer months at their second home in Huntington Beach. It was only natural for them to want to buy a boat. The summer house, which was also used as a hunting lodge in the winter, was built in 1926, the year his mother was born. Today, it is where T.K. and his own family live year-round. Oddly enough, T.K.'s grandfather's brother, who was a sea captain, had a daughter who now lives across the street from T.K.

It wasn't long before T.K.'s parents married. Arthur was in the armed forces at the time, and the two lived in the city before moving back to Huntington, where they lived above the shipyards. They then purchased a home on Bay Avenue and began to raise a family. Because they had twelve children, it became necessary to buy a bigger house. The old John Green House, circa 1890, was for sale on East Shore Road, although it was badly in need of repair. T.K. believes the oldest part of the house — the middle section — was built in 1820, although Historical Society records do not list an exact date of initial construction. Whatever the case may be, the Knutsons purchased it in 1962 and immediately began renovations. A year later they were able to move in. The house was appropriately named "East Point," and T.K. remembered many happy times there with his brothers and sisters.

"Previously, when we lived at the Bay Avenue house, we had lots of animals," T.K. recalled. "Five hundred chickens, and goats, pigs and cows.It was rough when we were young. We had some hard times until I was about fifteen years old."

"We loved the water though," he continued, "and as things got better and we moved to East Point, we all took sailing lessons. Eventually, we all had our own boats, but in order for us to get a two or three horsepower outboard, we had to be able to row from the house to the marina without stopping, and we had to be able to swim. We also had to be able to sail before we could have a power boat. We had to know everything."

As they got older, the Knutson children became so good at sailing that they began entering competitions. T.K. remembered racing on Long Island Sound as a child. It was a hobby he enjoyed for years. Fishing was also a major pastime at the Knutson house, although T.K. admits he found it pretty boring.

"My mother loved it, and she always took us fishing," T.K. said. "I liked clamming, though; that was my thing. My mother ate clams all year round. She would pull out a rowboat and go fishing or clamming off the property. I remember we made our own fishing hole with the carcasses and shells, and we'd make a pit where the fish would come and feed. There were plenty of fish then. We even got shrimp off the beach."

T.K.'s mother's family had an interesting history as well. His mother was English, not Norwegian, and her family were originally furniture makers. The Blue Room in the White House used to have some of her family's chairs. Her grandfather came to this country aboard the famous sailing vessel *Charles W. Morgan,* now restored and located at Mystic, Connecticut.

As the Knutson children got older and began to move out of the home they had grown to love, East Point became much too large for T.K.'s parents to live in and maintain. About 1974 Arthur Knutson purchased a smaller house, complete with a marina, in Cold Spring Harbor. The house was built during the Civil War, and had been owned by a church before the Knutsons bought it. The little marina had at one time been a whaler's boatyard. T.K.'s father would bring his boat right up to the house, located on Harbor Road. His father died in 1993, but his mother Ruth is still alive. She remains in the house and visits her children and twenty-six grandchildren. The old yard was sold to the Cold Spring Harbor Labs, and the shipbuilding businesses in Huntington continued to be run by the Knutson sons. At the time of his father's death, T.K.'s parents had been married almost fifty years. Sharing a wonderful life together, his parents and his grandmother on his father's side even shared the same birthday, August 30th.

By the time the Knutsons moved out of East Point, T.K. was on his way to a restaurant career. He spent the first few years working and learning the business, and by 1979 he opened T.K.'s Galley, in the vicinity of the family shipbuilding business.

"I didn't want to run the show like my brothers," T.K. said. "I wanted to do something different.." I asked why he thinks his restaurant is successful, when many restaurants come and go. "I cater to all ages, and people can come back and see people they haven't seen for a while," he replied. "There's a home atmosphere here, and it's very American. Everyone working here has something American in him. I think America's the finest place in the world — and I've been all over the world. There is just no place like it for freedom, or anything else." He paused. "Another thing that has made my place work is the homey atmosphere, the homemade soups, and bringing people back to the original food they can't find anyplace else. I have customers who have come here regularly every week since I opened." Not only have the locals enjoyed T.K.'s, but the place has seen such famous people as Billy Joel, the Bee Gees, and the Islanders.

T.K. has also been managing and maintaining properties for ten years in Halesite and Huntington. Eventually, when he retires from the restaurant business, he'd like to do more of this work. As a hobby, he says, "I'm big into outboarding, and I love collecting motors and antique cars." Like the rest of his brothers and sisters, T.K. still enjoys the water, and takes boat trips with his own family throughout the year.

The Knutson shipbuilding heritage continues in Halesite today. Along New York Avenue and East and West Shore Roads, the Knutson name is proudly displayed. The Knutson Marine Center, the Knutson Marine Store, Sport Boats, the Knutson Shipyard and Knutson's West Marine, are all owned and managed by some of T.K.'s brothers. Even his sisters lend a hand with the business when they can.

The Knutson Marina off East Shore Road in Halesite

T.K., his wife Elizabeth and their two children have no plans to leave Huntington, or the harbor they love. "Huntington, and especially Halesite, are places that everyone will keep coming back to," T.K. concluded. "It's all been built by hard work. To me, it is still a little fishing town, although it has grown tremendously. We have the most protected harbor on Long Island. I have so many good memories of things that *were* here and that I'm glad to say are *still* here."

HUNTINGTON BAY

"EAST POINT" AND THE STORY OF HETTY GREEN

The story of the Knutson family and the house they named "East Point" is told in the Halesite section of this book. Further information has been gathered from Town records, from Torkel Knutson and from the home's present owner, Mrs. Gloria Nostrand (formerly, and referred to here as, Mrs. Gloria Smith). Here is the history of this wonderful house, and of a most unusual woman who lived there.

Listed in historic records as the John Green House, this National Register Home was built circa 1890 on three acres along East Shore Road in Huntington Bay. The property is situated on the southernmost tip of a spit of land that juts into Huntington Harbor, and is part of the East Shore Road Historic District. The house is a significant example of the large, upper-income single family homes built in this incorporated village at the turn of the century.

The house offers spectacular views of the harbor, and is a distinctive example of the Colonial Revival style of architecture. It is a large, rambling 2½ story, gable-roofed house. It has three-bay, two-story, gambrel-roofed side wings and a very large five-bay, gable-roofed rear wing with a two-story tower. On the south facade, floor-to-ceiling windows flank the central entrance and open onto a beautiful Doric-columned veranda, or porch. The porch wraps around on the east side to form a port-cochere. The house has interior end chimneys, six-over-one windows, and gable dormers with multi-paned casement windows dominating the facade roof.

The house is said to have been built and lived in by a John Green, although there is no additional information in Town or Historical Society records. The records do refer to the house as the John Green House, or "Point Siesta." It was definitely lived in, however, by a mem-

134

ber of the Green family, Henrietta, otherwise known as "The Witch of Wall Street." Whether the house was built by her, or possibly a relative who may have been named John, is unclear. Henrietta's husband's name was Edward. In any event, the home's current owner, Gloria (Smith) Nostrand, has done research on the famous and unusual woman who once owned her house.

East Point, in Huntington Bay

Henrietta "Hetty" Green was born into a wealthy New Bedford, Massachusetts family in 1835. As a young girl, Hetty would go to Wall Street with her father, where she became very interested in the stock market. She had inherited over a million dollars from her family, and began buying stock. Hetty managed to make her money grow into a huge fortune. Shortly afterwards, she married millionaire Edward Green, and had two children, while living in the house on East Shore Road.

Through her shrewd investments, the money just kept coming. The more money she'd make, the less she'd spend. She became one of the country's wealthiest women, while at the same time "one of history's greatest tightwads." Numerous newspaper and magazine articles on Hetty's stinginess appeared, many of which are displayed in large frames in Gloria Smith's den. She has collected every article or photo she can find on the woman, because the story of her life is so bizarre.

The rise and fall of the stock market would greatly depend on Hetty's ever-changing moods. If she was in a bad mood, she would threaten to pull out all her investments, sending stockbrokers scrambling. She refused to eat in restaurants, and it is said her diet consisted mainly of graham crackers. If she had to stay overnight on Wall Street, she'd sleep in the park because she was too cheap to spend money on a hotel. Hetty always wore a long and very old black dress that people said was rotting. She never bought herself clothes. Every day, Hetty could be seen in the same black dress, with her hair tightly pulled up. She wore tall, black rubber boots which were literally stuffed with millions of dollars' worth of cash and securities.

Hetty trusted no one. If she was in a place where no one recognized her, Hetty would often go by a different name and pretend to be a pauper. By the looks of her, it was quite convincing, and she often got away without paying for things. By the time someone would find out who she was, she was gone. She even refused to pay for a two-dollar dog license, which of course she had previously registered under a different name.

Probably the most tragic example of Hetty's miserliness occurred when her young son Ned got into a terrible sledding accident one winter. In her tattered dress, she took her son (who was also dressed like a pauper) to a doctor. Under an alias, she told the doctor she had no money for treatments. However, the doctor soon realized who she was. He told Hetty her son had developed gangrene in his leg because she had waited so long to bring him in. If treatments were not given immediately, the gangrene would spread and his leg would need to be amputated. But even in the case of her son, Hetty was just too cheap. She refused to have him treated, and he lost his leg. The local newspapers went wild with the story.

Her husband Edward had had enough at this point. For years he and Hetty had battled over money, and she would often accuse him of being a spendthrift. What she did to their son was the last straw. He left Hetty, who was then fifty years old, in 1885. She was glad to see him go, and managed to get every bit of money he had as well. Edward died in 1902, with only a gold watch and seven dollars to his name.

Henrietta Green, America's wealthiest woman, died at East Point in 1916, at the age of eighty-one. She had suffered a stroke after arguing with someone in the house about money, and she burst a blood vessel in her neck from all the screaming. She died almost immediately, and left behind a one-hundred-million-dollar fortune.

As for her children, Ned and Sylvia, they inherited half of their mother's money. The one-legged Ned moved to Florida, where he became a spendthrift playboy, purchasing million-dollar yachts, private railroad cars and diamond-studded chamber pots. After spending an average of three million dollars a year, he died in 1936, weighing over three hundred pounds.

Daughter Sylvia had no use for her share of Hetty's money, because several years before Hetty's death she had convinced Sylvia to become a nun. Why? Nuns did not have to pay room and board.

Exactly what happened to the house after Hetty Green's death is unclear. It had several owners, but was eventually boarded up and abandoned in 1952. The once magnificent home remained empty, and greatly damaged, until 1962 when the Knutson family purchased it. Because of the terrible condition of the old house, Arthur Knutson paid practically nothing for it. He did, however, spend a year fixing it up before he and his family could live in it. The Knutsons spent many happy years there, and as times got better, Mr. Knutson updated the house and even put in a swimming pool. As the children grew up and moved out, the house became too large for Mr. and Mrs. Knutson alone, and they put East Point on the real estate market about 1974.

The house was very large and the taxes very high. For close to five years it was up for sale. Once again the beautiful home, without constant upkeep, began to deteriorate. It would take a very special person to buy the house and bring it back to its previous glory.

That person finally came along. For years, when Gloria Smith and her husband went by boat through Huntington Harbor, Gloria always stopped to stare at the magnificent house as they passed by. Jokingly, she would always say, "That's my house." When she discovered it had been on the market, she immediately had to see it. To her dismay, the long-vacant house was a disaster. The pipes had burst, and the first floor was under a foot of water. Raccoons and other wildlife had broken through and taken over the house. Mr. Smith had seen enough, and was quite happy to return to their home on Young's Hill Road. Mrs. Smith had other ideas. She agreed that the condition of the building was terrible, but it was the house she had dreamed of, and she was determined to get it and fix it up.

"Everyone thought I was out of my mind," Gloria said. "I mean, was I blind? It took a lot of convincing to get my husband to buy it, and when we finally did, we certainly had a lot of fights. We almost got divorced over it."

Mr. Smith stuck through it with his wife, despite all the time, money and nightmares involved. Even Mr. Knutson was saddened and apologetic for the state in which the house had fallen, and helped the Smiths as much as he could.

"I remember it wasn't long after we purchased the house that my daughter and her boyfriend came home from college," Gloria said. "We hadn't moved in yet and were still doing the renovations. I was excited to show it to her, though. My daughter saw the living room and then the kitchen. She wouldn't even let her boyfriend take a look. She turned around and told me I was crazy. Everyone said that. There were definitely times I thought they were right. I remember breaking down in tears once and saying, 'What did I do? My poor husband!'"

By the time they did move in, the house still wasn't quite the way it should have been. The long windows and doors on the porch did not close properly. The Smiths awoke to a terrible racket one night, and discovered six raccoons fighting in their living room. They had no choice but to lock themselves in the bedroom until morning.

As if this wasn't enough, other strange phenomena began to occur. Both Gloria and her husband heard many odd noises. For a while, neither wanted to tell the other. Although they had never before believed in ghosts, both of them were contemplating the idea that the house might be haunted.

"That's all I had to say to my husband," Gloria remembered. "He was upset enough about the whole thing. The main sound we heard was a rocking chair going back and forth on the porch every single night. Never did we have a rocker on the porch."

Sitting back for a moment, Gloria continued. "One night my husband woke up and heard someone walking across the porch. He turned on all the lights and went downstairs and looked outside. There was a lot of dew on the porch, but no footprints. He told me he definitely heard someone walking there. The rocker, though — that was the biggest thing."

East Point's magnificent porch overlooking Huntington Harbor

Despite these strange incidents, Gloria loved the house. I asked Torkel Knutson whether his family had experienced anything unusual in the house. Without giving it a second thought, he told me the house was haunted. "It never really bothered anybody, though," T.K. said. "It was just kind of spooky at times. Strangers always thought twice before entering the house. Sometimes the windows would open and close on a breezeless day, or the piano would play."

I mentioned to Mrs. Smith what T.K. had told me. The Smiths had never experienced anything with the windows or with the piano, but she did laugh and say, "So that's why the Knutsons left us the piano."

However, there was a time when Mrs. Smith experienced something quite frightening. To this day, she still has second thoughts and doubts about what she experienced, although the image of what she saw has stayed with her.

At first she was hesitant to speak about it. "You'll think I'm crazy if I tell you this," she began. "I was in the den on the couch one night. I do so much work during the day, I was tired and fell asleep on the couch. Everyone else had gone to bed. I was sound asleep, when I woke up to a rustling sound. The sound that material makes. I opened my eyes and I could have sworn I saw a lady and a little girl. I jumped up and they were gone. I was afraid to go from here to the stairs and up. I sat frozen for about an hour." Pausing for a moment, she said, "I thought, I'm just going to go back to sleep. Maybe I'm dreaming or something. I went back to sleep, this time facing the couch. I don't know how long it was, but then I felt something brush by, and I quickly turned around and saw this lady and a little girl. I thought I must be crazy, but then I got the feeling that said, 'don't move.' It was during this time we were seriously considering moving. We were thinking we just couldn't do this house anymore. It was too much." She paused again. "After being here for about six months, my husband kept saying, 'Look, so-and-so wants to buy it. Let's sell this thing. We can't do it. People were right.' But after the incident, I told him we couldn't. I said, 'But I got a message.'" She laughed. "Anyhow, I must be crazy. We didn't move, though."

It was not long after that she began to take books on Hetty Green out of the library. When I asked Gloria if she could remember what the woman looked like, she told me she was wearing a long black dress. Neither figure had any facial features. Learning more about Hetty Green, she believed the image that she saw could possibly have been her.

"But I still think maybe it could have been a dream," said Gloria. "Whatever it was, though, the message was 'don't go.'"

Upon restoring the house, Gloria Smith discovered in the basement an enormous walk-in safe with a built-in lock. It was Hetty Green's safe. I had the chance to see it when Gloria took me for a tour around the house. The safe is so big that she uses it for extra storage.

When Gloria's husband Wesley died fourteen years ago, Gloria didn't know how she could afford to stay in the house. The taxes and heating costs were enormous. As fate would have it, several movie production companies and magazines discovered this one-of-a-kind house, and approached Mrs. Smith with the possibility of doing some shoots there. After some thought, Gloria agreed.

East Point had become quite an attraction. Since Gloria and her husband had totally renovated and beautifully decorated the once deteriorating home, everyone wanted to shoot there. The house has twenty-two completely restored spacious rooms, a 45-foot living room, banquet-size dining room, oak paneled library, huge country kitchen, a keeping room, a 34-foot master bedroom with outdoor balcony, seven other large bedrooms, eight working fireplaces, twelve-foot ceilings, and of course the wraparound porch. A private elevator leads to a third floor apartment with a balcony that offers a 270-degree panoramic view of Huntington Harbor. Elsewhere on the property is a separate cottage located at the water's edge, an antique children's playhouse, a 125-foot boat pier and 1500 feet of beach. The swimming pool, which measures 65 feet by 25 feet, has a 40-foot sun deck which extends high over the water's edge. It is truly an incredible house.

East Point has seen such celebrities as Lena Horne, Steve Allen, Carol Alt, Debbie Gibson, and Gloria's personal favorite, James Earl Jones. Jones did the very first Yellow Book ad at the house. Scenes from the movie "The Dogs of War" were filmed in her living room. Photographers from Vogue, Elle and Bride Magazine photographed models across the wonderful porch and by the luxurious pool. Even Publisher's Clearing House did a shoot there, showing the house as one of the things you could buy if you became a millionaire.

In the same room where the articles and photos of Hetty Green grace the walls, the opposite wall is filled with covers of magazines, and photos and autographs of stars. Gloria Smith, who takes care of most of the upkeep of the house herself, is thankful for the occasional extra income.

"I'll stay here as long as I can afford to," she said. "I live here with my second husband now, and two of my four daughters. I will always love this house."

After she and her first husband had made the decision to stay, she never experienced any ghostly phenomena again. Perhaps it had been Hetty, after all, who told her not to go.

She has kept the name East Point in honor of the Knutson family, whom she greatly respects and admires. She also refuses to remove the iron gate with the huge letter K in it, which leads to the pool. "A part of this house will always belong to the Knutsons" she said, "so I think that it should stay."

IS THIS MOTHER CHICK'S INN?

In writing about history, research is often the most difficult task. Many times I have found errors and contradictions in names, dates and places, and have to look further, hoping to verify what is correct. When it is not possible to prove something, I alert my readers. Regarding Mother Chick's Inn, the subject of this story, there are two conflicting accounts, neither of which can be proven.

Throughout Huntington's history, an old house on Bay Road in Huntington Bay has been referred to as Mother Chick's. Our late Town Historian, Rufus B. Langhans, even had a blue historical sign erected there, marking its place in history. When I went to see the home's owner in order to take a photograph for this story, he gave me a tour of the house and cited reasons why he doesn't believe it was ever Mother Chick's. It is an interesting tale either way, so I will present both sides and leave it up to you to decide whether or not it is the Mother Chick's Inn.

The historical marker states: *Mother Chick's Inn (Chichester) Reputed to be where Nathan Hale was betrayed on his fateful venture to New York City in September 1776.* Two books, one on Nathan Hale written in 1902, and one written on Huntington by Hon. Henry C. Platt in 1876, mentions old Mother Chick, also known as Mother Chich, Mother Chidd and Widow Chichester. She is said to have kept a tavern, "a rendezvous for the Tories of the neighborhood," during the time of the American Revolution. This house, which was taken over by the British and Tory soldiers, was located in a place called "The Cedars," (probably named for the many cedar trees there). No exact location or address is listed in either source.

A Building Structure Inventory Form from the Division for Historic Preservation, New York State Parks and Recreation in Albany, which was filed at the Huntington Historical Society in the summer of 1979, lists this house as Mother Chick's Inn-Johnson Farm. It notes that it is a 1½ story, three-bay gable roof house which faces south. It is of saltbox profile, and it has an interior chimney at the west end. Item number 20 on the form states the following: *This important early house has been carefully restored and is well cared for. It is probably "Mother Chick's Inn," an 18th century tavern, where Nathan Hale is thought to have hidden for a time after landing on the beach at the north end of the road that runs past this place.* It then goes on to list ownership, beginning in 1836 with the name Johnson. In 1858 an S. Johnson is listed as owner and in 1873 a Mrs. Johnson is listed as owner. It does not list any owners in the 1700's. Sources for this information were the archives of the Town of Huntington Historian's Office, and a U.S. Coast Survey from 1836, Rockville, Maryland. This survey lists it as *probably* Mother Chick's, and does not give any additional information to prove that it is. Records of the 18th century are often hard to come by, and this may be the reason why owners before 1836 are not listed.

Other research indicates that from the mid-1800's to 1928, there were a few owners, and some tenants in the house. The next owner, from 1928 until 1935, was Samuel Everett, who had been editor of *American Home* magazine. In the files at the Historical Society I found an April 1933 article from that magazine, written about the house. The writer was Samuel Everett's wife, Helen. In her article, "Reclaiming a Long Island Farmhouse," she refers to the house as just that — an old Long Island farmhouse, not as a tavern, and mentions Mother Chick's as being a separate house altogether. The following passage is from the article, which was written during the Everetts' ownership. (Note: I normally do not include such long quotations, but I felt this one was necessary in order to show both sides of the story).

The contour of the land was good. Hills sloped down to the house from the north and east. The house itself stood on a slight rise above the orchard, which deepened into woods at the south rim. A great black walnut tree stood guard on one side, and a fir on the other. They were striplings on the night when Nathan Hale knocked at the door of William Johnson's farmhouse to ask for a night's lodging. The conflicting tales about the spy seem to agree that this house is the one remaining landmark on Long Island which sheltered the gallant American when he went on the perilous mission which cost him his life. Its owner, William Johnson, was one of the few revolutionary sympathizers along this shore. Nathan Hale, at the outset of his journey to map General Howe's fortifications and forces about Brooklyn, crossed Long Island Sound from Connecticut to Huntington. Under cover of night, he reached the Johnson farm, and fortunately the master himself came to the door. Hale received not only a bed, but some valuable information before continuing his walk to Brooklyn. The story persists that he returned to Huntington and was captured from Mother Chick's Inn here while waiting for a boat to take him back to Connecticut. This is refuted, however, by the Order Book of General Howe, which mentions the capture on the night of September 21st and the execution at 11 o'clock the next day in front of Artillery Park, N.Y.

The article shows two photographs; one matches the photo I took for this book, and is listed as the Johnson house, and the other is of Mother Chick's Inn — Place of Nathan Hale's Discovery. Again, no address or exact location is noted.

When I arrived to take the photo of the Bay Road house, I met its owner, Ed Weinman, who disagrees that his house was the tavern of Mother Chick's. At this point, I did not mention the article quoted from above. I told him that the information I found through the Historical Society and the Town Historian's Office listed, and accepted, his house as being Mother Chick's. Mr. Weinman told me that his father, Hanus J. Weinman, had purchased the house in 1946. Ed grew up in the old house, and when his father died in 1978 he acquired it, along with seven acres that had been divided into three lots. Ed Weinman purchased an additional two acres of preserved land, totaling nine acres. Supposedly, the property at one time consisted of approximately twenty-three acres, (as mentioned in the Everett article).

Mr. Weinman spoke of the orchards which had once existed there, and he showed me the unique kettle hole, or glacial pond, located not far from the house. (According to the inventory report at the Historical Society, the kettle hole on the property is one of the best remnants of Long Island's glacial history). He pointed out the many tall trees surrounding the house and told me how the British would wait at Mother Chick's, at the head of Huntington Bay, and watch for the ships to come in. Grant the fact that many of the trees were not there then, or if they were, they were much smaller; however, the Everett article spoke of Mother Chick's being near enough to the water that boats could be seen coming ashore. The location of Mr. Weinman's house, he believes, is much too far away from the shore; since you can't see the harbor from there, how could the British see ships coming in?

Was this Mother Chick's Inn?

Upon taking the tour of the house, it was clear that the interior, even though it has been altered, showed no evidence of ever being an 18th century inn. Its layout, according to Mr. Weinman, was a typical saltbox farmhouse, (as also described by Everett). He stated that throughout the years people referred to his house as Mother Chick's tavern or inn, and so it became. Oral tradition does have some weight, but in this case, Mr. Weinman believes it is a mistaken identity which no longer can be corrected. He thinks Nathan Hale may have stayed here a night or two, but again, there is no proof. He spoke to the late Rufus Langhans on many an occasion regarding the conflicting stories, and about the possibility of changing or removing the historic marker. He believes it misrepresents history, but Mr. Langhans would hear nothing of it, insisting it was Mother Chick's.

Mr. Weinman believes the real Mother Chick's Inn is located at the end of Vineyard Road, in a house where his father once knew the owner. He remembered going to the house on Vineyard when his father was alive, and they spoke of the possibility of it being Mother Chick's. Its location on the harbor, with its breathtaking views, would have been perfect for the British to see incoming ships. The house has been changed over the years, but Mr. Weinman claimed the original part, with its old beams and huge central fireplace, was the perfect layout for an inn or tavern.

The information Ed Weinman had given me made sense, but on the other hand he had no written or physical evidence to support his idea. I took things a step further and went back to the Historical Society to get any information I could on the house on Vineyard Road.

The only information they had was another Building-Structure Inventory Form from 1979. It listed its date of the original structure as c. 1790. Perhaps it was built prior to that year. It described the house as being a three-bay, 2½ story clapboard gable roofed house with two end chimneys. It had a one-story shed-roofed porch across the back, and a 1½ story gable-roofed wing on the east side, with a shed-roofed dormer and one end chimney. Alterations had been made in 1947, when a section was added to the original house, and in 1950, when dormers were added to the second story of the original section. Records lists Widow Fleet owning it in 1858, and that it existed in 1836, although no owner is listed. If you refer to the description of Mr. Weinman's house on the inventory done in 1979, both houses have very similar characteristics. Could the two houses have been mistaken for each other? The photo of the Vineyard Road house in the survey contained the additions. If you look at the original part of the house, however, it looks almost exactly like the photo of Mother Chick's Inn in the Everett article, with the exception of the chimney being on the opposite end of the house.

I made one last attempt, and contacted the current owners of the Vineyard Road house, who were very much interested in the information I gave them, but had no answers. They had never even heard a rumor that their house could have been Mother Chick's. The owner did tell me, however, that the house had been greatly altered on the interior as well as the exterior, and that five fireplaces were currently in the house. None were the one Ed Weinman had described, but the Vineyard Lane owner didn't doubt that it had existed there at one time.

So the question remains ... which house is the Mother Chick's Inn? You be the judge.

THE RUINS OF FERGUSON'S CASTLE

"What's old collapses, times change, and new life blossoms in the ruins."

—*Johann Christoph Friedrich von Schiller*
1759-1806

As mentioned in the preface, the idea behind my work is to elicit public awareness and appreciation of Huntington's history. Therefore, the places and structures written about in this book still exist, and should be preserved. However, I felt it was important to include one place that no longer exists: the great Ferguson's Castle, also known as The Monastery. The only thing remaining of this incredible castle, once located in the hills of Huntington Bay, are the ruins along East Shore Road.

I wanted to include its story for two reasons: it has a wonderful and interesting history, and it may serve as a lesson for us all. In the type of work I do, I have the opportunity to meet and interview many interesting people. I cannot tell you how many of these people have mentioned Ferguson's Castle to me, and the awful fate that befell it in 1970. It surprised me to learn how distraught people were over the destruction of this building. As I began to research it, I realized it was a terrible loss, one that can never be replaced. With so many organizations fighting to save Huntington's historic structures today, it's a shame they weren't as successful years ago. Perhaps Ferguson's Castle could have been saved.

Miss Juliana Armour, daughter of Herman Ogden Armour, who was the founder of the famous Armour Meat Company, married Dr. Farquhar Ferguson, a New York City pathologist, in the late 1800's. It was the couple's dream to build a great castle where they could raise their seven children.

Mrs. Ferguson was a convert to Catholicism, and while traveling in Europe, fell in love with the magnificent monasteries there. It was then that they decided the castle would be a "monastery" of their own. Land had been chosen on Long Island's exclusive North Shore, on the hills overlooking Huntington Harbor, in the area we know today as Huntington Bay. The Fergusons purchased thirteen and a half acres near the famous Fanny Brice/Nick Arnstein home, and plans were drawn up and designed by Allen W. Jackson of Boston.

However, Dr. Ferguson died quite young and rather unexpectedly, before the construction began. Not long after, the widowed Mrs. Ferguson decided, in her husband's memory, to carry out the dream they had shared.

It was 1908 when the Webster and Smith Construction Company of Boston began construction of what Mrs. Ferguson called "The Monastery." She wanted her home and gardens to have a religious feeling and theme, and she began establishing an enormous monastic art collection, the finest money could buy, while construction of the home was taking place.

It was important that Mrs. Ferguson be available to oversee construction of The Monastery, so she rented two floors at the nearby Edgewater Hotel, the place where the family had spent many a summer vacation. By 1911, the magnificent and unusual structure was complete. Mrs. Ferguson and her children, May, Juliana, Craigie, Armour, Danforth, Farquhar, Jr., and Wallace, moved into their new home on May 26.

The white stucco, Spanish/Italian style mansion contained forty rooms, six baths, fourteen fireplaces and many outdoor gardens, cloisters and patios. The house even had a chapel. The servant's wing alone consisted of eight bedrooms, one bath, a staff kitchen, laundry room, living room, and a cloistered porch that overlooked the harbor.

The Grand Hall was the largest room in the Castle and measured 64 feet in length, with a width of 47 feet. The room was illuminated by an enormous skylight that rose three stories above the floor and covered the entire room. Supported by hand-hewn oak beams that had been taken from the estate's woods, the skylights offered light by day and a star-studded sky at night, where the family sat and studied the constellations.

The Refectory was the most religious room in the house, and had the ambience of a church. Panel paintings depicting scenes from Christ's life were mounted on either side of a pair of doors which connected the Drawing Room to the Refectory. The room itself had high, vaulted arched ceilings painted in a mosaic-style fresco, portraying scenes from the Bible. It had been modeled after famous Early Byzantine mosaics that were found in churches and tombs in Italy. It took the renowned mural painter Robert Sewell of Oyster Bay four and a half years to complete the fresco, which measured 50 by 24 feet. The room also contained a Spanish-style carved marble fireplace. Pillars dating back to the time of the Crusades supported the heavy marble that rested on marble lions from the same period. Various other religious symbols and reliefs were located around the room, as well as in the leaded glass window. The floor was made of hand-set slate and was covered by a large Persian rug. On top of this was a long, oak table with matching chairs that had been taken from a medieval monastery in southern France.

The house was quite modern for its day. It contained an elevator, an automatic built-in vacuum cleaning system, an electric paging system, and most unique, a built-in clothes dryer that measured approximately 10 feet long, 8 feet high and 5 feet deep. Inside was a metal box where seven drawers were pulled out. The wet laundry was put onto rods that extended from the front to the back of the drawers, and which were pushed back into the metal box when loaded. Seven loads of laundry could be dried at once, and nothing ever had to be ironed.

Approaching the Monastery from the outside, visitors first passed the Gate House that still exists on East Shore Road, and which was modeled after a 17th century Spanish carriage house.

The old Gate House at Ferguson's Castle

A long driveway circled up toward the house between high cement walls, which were built to prevent erosion and to protect the Fergusons' privacy. Gargoyles, Gothic stone figures and bas-relief carvings were embedded in and around the cement walls that surrounded the driveway and castle. At the top of the driveway, the area widened into a large, gardened entrance courtyard that also contained many priceless statues. Above, the huge stone tower made of authentic Spanish tile was the place where the Ferguson family retreated to marvel at the spectacular view of the harbor. Part of the old cement wall and some small statues can still be seen today, although instead of looking up at a tower and a castle, a very modern home stands in its place. However, it isn't difficult to picture the magnificent castle that once existed there. Elsewhere on the property had been a stable full of ponies for the children, swimming pools, a 110-foot yacht, a garage, and of course, the beach.

Part of the old walls of Ferguson's Castle, with modern house above

Just as interesting as the castle, and very entertaining, is the story of Mrs. Ferguson's life with her family. Mrs. Ferguson was quite the opposite of the miserly Hetty Green of East Point. She was generous to the extreme. Her children were her entire life, and she seemed to love everyone else's children as much as her own. Her five boys were quite rambunctious, while the two girls were a bit more reserved. No matter what her children did, nothing seemed to faze Mrs. Ferguson.

The home was the site of many gala parties. Guests were always present at The Monastery, but oddly enough, they were usually friends of the children and not Mrs. Ferguson's own friends, whom she seldom entertained. She wanted her home to be filled with the sounds and laughter of children playing. As her children grew and began working in the city, Mrs. Ferguson insisted her children drive their friends home with them. If they returned without them, it is said she often sent them back to the city to pick them up. The ponies were accessible to her guests, as well as the boat. Everything in the garage, from bicycles to motorcycles to cars, were offered to her own children, and believe it or not, to all the children in the neighborhood. Her garage was open twenty-four hours a day so that anyone could have access to the vehicles. No one ever stole anything, since they were always available. If one of her sons wanted a car or motorcycle and so did one of his friends, she purchased another. She would end up buying two of everything.

Mrs. Ferguson was indeed a millionaire, but according to her neighbors she was in no way pretentious, nor did she do anything out of charity, only love. One time, a child in the neighborhood was going blind and required an eye specialist. The boy's parents could not afford the services of a doctor. Mrs. Ferguson found out about the matter, and paid for the boy to see a specialist in New York City. The boy was operated on and was completely cured.

It was not unusual to see the children using the Grand Hall as a roller skating rink, or jumping from the balconies onto the plush furnishings. The house was always filled with animals as well, who had full rein in the house, including the furniture. The animals joined guests in the Refectory, even at the fanciest of parties. The family pets included ponies, chickens, a raccoon, two Great Danes, a spitz, and four Boston bulldogs.

Food was served throughout the day. Mrs. Ferguson had two Japanese servants whose only job was to keep the long table in the Refectory filled with food at all times, in case any of the children or their friends were hungry.

As far as the children's expenses were concerned, they could buy whatever they wanted. All of Huntington's merchants had expense accounts for the Ferguson children. A secretary was hired by Mrs. Ferguson specifically to keep track of the children's expenses and to pay their accounts.

Winters were a favorite time in the Ferguson family, despite the fact that it took more than nine and a half tons of coal to heat the Castle each day. Mrs. Ferguson would hitch up a horse and sleigh and ride all over Huntington, with her children following behind on a bobsled. Mrs. Ferguson especially loved Christmas, and every Christmas Eve she would drive to New York City and give out presents to every police officer she could find. Everyone in Huntington could not help but love Mrs. Ferguson.

As wonderful as she was, she wasn't without her oddities. Boxing with the children was one of her favorite pastimes. So was collecting foreign tombstones that had marked the graves of young children. The stones were all over 300 years old, and she used them as decorative pieces throughout the house. Some were placed on the walls or floors, while others were located above the bedroom doors. She even made tables and benches with them, to be used in the garden and cloister areas. She also had an obsession with the number twenty-one. A pond was stocked with twenty-one goldfish and twenty-one turtles. She used the number wherever she could. Oddly enough, Mrs. Ferguson died in the year 1921.

She spent many happy years at the Castle with her children. But eventually the time came that she had been dreading: her children became adults and moved out to start lives of their own. This was a difficult and unhappy time for Mrs. Ferguson, who suffered immense loneliness. She spent some time in her New York City home, at 36 West Fifty-Ninth Street, but kept coming back to Huntington. She considered selling The Monastery several times, but could never bear to do it. She could not part with her dream castle and all the happy memories she had there.

Her son Armour had married and moved out in 1913. With the approach of World War I, Farquhar, Jr. joined the Lafayette Escadrille, while Danforth joined the American Expeditionary Force. Craigie joined the fliers in Canada, and Wallace, her youngest son, was living upstate, possibly attending school. May had married Alfred Marshall, and Juliana moved out to begin her own life.

As if things weren't difficult enough, Mrs. Ferguson received news in 1919 that almost destroyed her. Wallace, after a two-week illness, died of influenza on October 16. A month later, Mrs. Ferguson got word that Danforth had died on the front lines in France just four days after his brother's death. To make matters worse, in July of 1920, Armour and his wife filed a divorce suit which resulted in rumors and scandal.

All this was more than Mrs. Ferguson could handle, and she went "off the deep end," so to speak. It was said that being so distraught over Wallace's death, she had a wax dummy made in his likeness that was wheeled to the Refectory every evening for dinner. The table was set for two: Mrs. Ferguson, who dressed in flowing evening gowns, and the wax figure of Wallace, who was also dressed in evening clothes. Not long after, Mrs. Ferguson was stricken with a terrible cancer, sarcomatosis of the intestines. She died heartbroken on November 27, 1921, at the age of fifty-six. Three days later, Armour's divorce was finalized.

The children had squandered the family's money, and they could no longer afford the upkeep on the Castle. It was put on the market, and in 1922 the Manhattan Greer School for Girls purchased it. However, the cost of maintenance, as well as its distant location from the city, caused the school to close shortly thereafter.

The fate of Ferguson's Castle then took many turns. It was purchased in 1926 by a retired Buffalo publisher, William J. Conners, who did little to alter it except for transforming the chapel into a gymnasium, and removing all the tombstones scattered about the house. Upon his death, ownership of the estate kept changing hands time and time again.

By 1936, The Ferguson children auctioned off most of the contents of "The Monastery" in the hopes of raising money. Millions of dollars worth of precious art and furnishings were sold for practically nothing. A grand chariot carved in ivory and set with rubies, costing over $50,000, was sold for only $6,250. In a two-week period, a total of 2,385 items were auctioned.

The following year, The Monastery was purchased by Charles Cords, a Brooklyn attorney, who used the house mainly on weekends and in the summer. Unlike Mrs. Ferguson, Mr. Cords was a very private person. Visitors were rare at the Castle.

By 1964, the cost of living, which included maintaining the Castle, was on the rise, and Mr. Cords and his wife could no longer afford to stay there. Mr. Cords was terribly upset about leaving, and died only a month later. With $100,000 in unpaid back taxes, Suffolk County took possession of the estate and put it up for auction several times, without any luck. Soon, vandalism and neglect took over the once magnificent home. What few priceless statues and art remained were either stolen or destroyed. The Castle, where so many children had laughed and played, was abandoned. The beautiful architecture, shown in movies filmed during the Fergusons' time, was ruined.

Lionel Barrymore and Grace Valentine had been at the Castle during the filming of the movie "A Brand of Cowardice." The other movie filmed there was "Romeo and Juliet" in 1916, produced by the Metro Company, later Metro-Goldwyn-Mayer, and starring Francis X. Bushman and Beverly Bayne.

In June of 1970, Ferguson's Castle, was demolished. Only the ruins along East Shore Road remained. Not long afterward, several new homes were built on the site.

The owners following the Fergusons, while living in the old Castle, had revealed some "haunting" information. Supposedly, for years the ghost of Mrs. Ferguson could be seen floating down the staircase to the Refectory every evening. She was dressed in her usual flowing evening gown.

At a lecture I attended in the fall of 1995, the topic of Ferguson's Castle was discussed, including Mrs. Ferguson's ghostly appearances after her death. Perhaps even in spirit Mrs. Ferguson could not leave behind the place she loved so much. I have even heard a rumor that the many homes located on the old site contain a ghostly presence from the past that no one can quite explain.

CENTERPORT

CENTERPORT'S FAMOUS LITTLE COTTAGE: THE HOME OF ARTHUR DOVE

When Centerport comes to mind, many people think of Vanderbilt's Gold Coast mansion or the town's earliest settlers, the Suydams, while still others think of the hilltop streets, the beautiful beaches and the fine restaurants. Centerport (spelled Centreport in earlier times) was formerly called Little Cow Harbor. It was named for its location in the center of the north shore of Huntington, the "port" being "centered" between the east and west boundaries of the Town. What many people don't know about, however, is the tiny cottage which quietly overlooks the serene Mill Pond on Centerport's Centershore Road. Located directly across from the Centerport Post Office, the little house has served as a general store, a post office and as the home of a famous abstract painter, Arthur Dove.

The neatly-kept dwelling is today the chiropractic office of Dr. Lisa Conway, Mill Pond Chiropractic. The structure was in very poor condition when Dr. Conway purchased it two years ago. Much time and effort went into restoring the tiny building, which has a wonderful history dating back to the 1800's.

It was first known as the Benham's General Store, circa 1880. The store sold a multitude of items from homemade remedies for people and horses, to groceries, hardware and ice cream. Early post offices were generally located in these types of stores, and Benham's was no exception. The postmaster/proprietor handled the mail as well as selling the store's goods. Those who lived on the opposite side of the pond were often seen rowing a boat to the store/post office. This was usually faster than walking or hitching up a horse. Eventually the General Store closed and was left abandoned until it was purchased in 1938 by painter Arthur Dove, who lived there until his death in 1946. Because of Dove's contributions and recognition in the art world, the house is best known as The Arthur Dove Home. (A blue historical marker depicts the site as Dove's).

Born in 1880 in Canandaigua, New York, Arthur Dove was known as the country's first modern painter, and was influential in promoting awareness of abstract art. His works were rarely literal, and some of his most important paintings were created in the little cottage.

Originally an illustrator, Dove abandoned his career and went to Paris in 1907 to become a painter. Remarkably, in the course of two short years Dove had absorbed the entirety of modern European art. His works became primarily nonobjective images, although some had a hint of subject matter, such as a suggestion of a building or landscape. The 1910 paintings which he entitled "Abstractions" became well known.

Eventually, Arthur Dove felt the need to return to a greater degree of representation. Generally, though, he was concerned more with the spiritual forces of nature than with its external forms. He transformed the natural forms and objects into colorful geometric and abstract designs. For instance, he would evoke the sensation of the wind blowing over a hill without actually painting the hill or the wind. His ideas of "non-realistic" artistic expression differed greatly from what was popular during that era. Many said he was far ahead of his time.

Shortly after this change of artistic style, Dove had a number of personal problems, including a separation from his wife and son. By 1920 he met another artist, Helen Torr (nicknamed "Reds"), and he began living and painting with her. They lived on a houseboat which was anchored in the Harlem River. Money was always a problem, and this was all they could afford at the time. Artists such as John Marin and Georgia O'Keefe often received $6,000 for one painting, while Dove received only a few hundred dollars if in fact a buyer could be found.

Nevertheless, by 1923 Dove had enough money to buy a used 42-foot yawl. It was on this vessel, which they called "Mona," that Dove and Torr lived, painted and cruised Long Island Sound. By 1925 they were married and became "house-sitters" at the Ketewomoke Yacht Club in Halesite, in exchange for free rent, all the while painting and discovering new ideas.

Although Dove's true interests lay in American Romanticism, like many American artists he was greatly influenced by European Surrealism during the 1920's. During the 1930's this influence grew. He transformed landscapes into monsters, or the sun or moon into a giant Cyclops' eye. In 1938, he purchased the little abandoned cottage on Centerport's Mill Pond. He painted colorful and poetic impressions of what he viewed from the small back porch which faced the pond.

Arthur Dove's Centerport cottage

His work changed very little until the 1940's, when he experimented with geometric abstraction. Stricken at this time with Bright's disease, and trying to recover from a heart attack, the ailing Dove continued to do what he loved best—painting. He was so weak at times that his wife had to support his hand, but he was constantly inspired by the beautiful country views surrounding his home.

Four years before his death, he painted what was called "Square on the Pond." The work was inspired by the peaked roofs of the old Chalmers House which stood across the water. The Chalmers House, originally the area's largest hotel, was purchased in 1888 by the Order of Franciscan Brothers as a summer home. Circa 1904, the Brothers added the second tower which formed "the peaks" that Dove illustrated in his painting. The Chalmers House was then known as Mount Alvernia. Today it is Camp Alvernia, and it is the oldest Catholic summer camp in the nation.

It was sights such as these that influenced Arthur Dove. From his bed, Dove still used his imagination as he looked out his window, watching the sea gulls swoop toward the water. He said, "Their beaks look like ivory thrown slowly through space."

Until his death in 1946, Dove remained a true artist. He worked from deep within his soul and expressed himself through paint on canvas. The little cottage remains a symbol of the gentle painter. Although no ghost has ever appeared there, Dr. Conway's patients say there is a very calm and peaceful feeling about the place. Perhaps it is Dove, showing his approval of what had become of his favorite spot by the harbor.

THE ESTATE OF WILLIAM KISSAM VANDERBILT II

Yachts, auto racing, cultural artifacts, natural history and marine specimens, priceless art, history, golf, architecture, antiques and astronomy were just some of the things which interested one of Long Island's richest men, William Kissam Vanderbilt II.

Born into a family of wealth in 1878, William K. Vanderbilt II was the great-grandson of Cornelius Vanderbilt, founder of the New York Central Railroad and the Staten Island Ferry. At his death in 1887, Cornelius' fortune was estimated at $100 million. Following in his footsteps, William II became vice president and then president of the railroad, with offices in New York City. He was also one of the major philanthropic and civic leaders of the early twentieth century.

William was also quite involved on Long Island, where he built the high speed Long Island Motor Parkway, created to encourage American car companies to keep pace with European car design. Known as "Willie K.," Vanderbilt's passion was motor car racing, and his home displayed a vast number of trophies and awards. He was also an avid sailor and a master mariner, owning several large ships and yachts which he used for touring the world. He visited such exotic places as Polynesia, the Galapagos Island and Australia.

William K. Vanderbilt II was married to Virginia Fair, heiress to the Comstock Lode, for seven years, and had three children: two girls, Muriel and Consuelo, and a son, William K. Vanderbilt III. He and Virginia then divorced, and he looked for what he called a "bachelor retreat".

It was 1906 when Vanderbilt found a 43-acre plot in Centerport, overlooking Northport Harbor, Long Island Sound and the Connecticut shoreline. The location suited his needs very well, because it offered suitable anchorage for his yachts, and provided proximity to the racetrack. His most powerful and largest yacht would often be seen docked there. The yacht was named *Alva* after William's mother.

The original home on the property was a small six-room Japanese style summer house. Through the years, the house was greatly enlarged and extensively remodeled by the renowned New York architectural firm of Warren and Wetmore, and by a lesser-known architect, Ronald H. Pearce. By 1928, the little house had been transformed into a three story, 24-room Spanish Baroque style mansion — a style popular in the early twentieth century — and was filled with rare and unusual objects.

The huge iron entrance gates to the estate were taken from William's father's Oakdale mansion, known as Idle Hour. Two great iron eagles, which once stood atop Grand Central Station in New York, are just beyond the gates and guard the entrance to the mansion. A cobblestone driveway leads first to six columns of sculptured Cipalino marble from the ruins of Carthage, and then to the mansion, which is appropriately called "Eagle's Nest." Before entering the central courtyard, which is intricately paved with Belgian blocks, the driveway crosses a bridge and curves to reveal a great stone archway surmounted by a bell tower containing bells made in 1715. An ancient clock tower can also be seen. Surrounding the house and courtyard are beautiful, multi-colored mosaic walks inspired by the walks of Madeira, and 180 linden trees imported from Germany.

With a mix of southern European influences, the Spanish Baroque style home features characteristic stucco wall surfaces, arcades, red tile roofs, arched entrances, wrought-iron window grilles, shaded ornamental balcony railings, ornate plaster reliefs, decorative fountains and a main courtyard cloister.

Multiple scallop shell images are carved on many doors and posts, and can also be seen in the limestone walls. According to old sea lore, the shell brought good luck.

The entrance to the estate, which is now the Vanderbilt Museum

The interior of the house is just as elaborate and ornate as the outside. It contains furnishings and art from all over the world, and from many time periods. Enormous family portraits line many of the hallways. During the 1930's, Warren and Wetmore added a museum wing to the house, and also enlarged another museum building known as "Hall of Fishes," located elsewhere on the property.

Many of the rooms are open to the public today, through tours given by Vanderbilt Museum tour guides. The dining room is decorated in a Spanish-Moroccan motif, and has tiled flooring, carved wooden ceilings and rough white walls. Old Moorish weapons inlaid with silver, ivory and jewels are hung throughout the room. The furniture is Italian Renaissance, in a monastery style. The furniture includes a carved walnut alms counter with two offering slots, twelve carved walnut side chairs covered in 17th century Flemish leather, an eleven-foot 17th century Florentine refectory table of carved walnut, and a corner fireplace with a tiled Vanderbilt coat of arms over it.

The sitting room contains 13th century Portuguese handiwork, as well as a Portuguese fireplace dated 1491. It was not uncommon for William Vanderbilt to bring back large artifacts, even whole walls, from other countries — usually carried on one of his yachts. The Organ Room was one such room, in which the walls were reconstructed in his home. The room contained a 1,000-wood-and-metal pipe Aeolian organ which cost Vanderbilt $90,000. Also in the room are 15th century oil paintings, a Caen mantle and fireplace, a Persian Kurd rug and a carved oak archbishop's chair on a dais. An Elizabethan style oak refectory table contains Vanderbilt memorabilia, and a guest book on the table contains the signatures of many famous people, including the Duke and Duchess of Windsor.

At one point, William had a special room made for his ex-wife, Virginia, in the hope she would return to him. The room, similar to that of a French Chateau, was never visited by her. He and his second wife, Rosamond Lancaster Warburton, lived in the house, although they had separate bedrooms. Mr. Vanderbilt's room overlooked the courtyard on one side and the harbor on the other. It was furnished in the French Empire style, reminiscent of Napoleon, whom Vanderbilt greatly admired. A breakfast room overlooking the pool connected Vanderbilt's bedroom to his wife's bedroom, which was of Georgian architecture and design. Most impressive was her bathtub, hewn from a solid block of marble and adorned with solid gold fixtures.

The Memorial Room was added in 1936 and contains a display of African big game brought back from the Anglo-Egyptian Sudan by Mr. Vanderbilt's only son, William K. Vanderbilt III, while on safari in 1931. The room was dedicated to his son, who died in a car accident in 1933 at the age of twenty-seven. Vanderbilt believed the dramatic room was a fitting tribute.

The museum wings were added to the mansion during and after Vanderbilt's stay there, and serve a wide variety of purposes. Vanderbilt wanted to share everything he saw and collected with others, and said his home would be "for the use, education and enjoyment of the public." This was a philosophy he lived by.

The Memorial Wing contains a scale model of the yacht *Alva*, as well as a multitude of exhibits such as a wonderful bird life display, folklore of the South Sea Islands, ship models, auto racing memorabilia and trophies, a weapons collection, and a fascinating group of nine marine life habitat exhibits.

The Habitat Room was designed to reflect a variety of habitats throughout the world, with each diorama depicting a different ecosystem. Subtle, bluish floor lighting suggests the impression of being under water, and enhances the feel of the exhibit.

The Stoll Wing is named after Charles H. Stoll, a former Trustee of the Vanderbilt Museum Commission. In keeping with William K. Vanderbilt II's philosophy, Stoll at age 80 donated a collection of wild animals, which were placed in beautifully painted dioramas depicting their habitats around the world.

The Guest Wing houses a 3,000-year-old mummy, and the Model Room contains a model of the mansion as it looked in the 1920's. The model was commissioned by Vanderbilt himself.

The Hall of Fishes was opened to the public in 1922, and was enlarged in the 1930's. The two-story building houses a huge collection of marine life which Vanderbilt collected and identified himself, and includes 40 specimens not previously discovered. The museum also features natural habitat groups, wildlife dioramas, game heads and stuffed tropical birds. The top of the roof was actually the first tee of Vanderbilt's private golf course.

The rest of the great Vanderbilt estate includes a boathouse, a sea plane hangar, a power house and garage complex, a carriage house (now the Imagination Station), a curator's cottage, and the famous Vanderbilt Planetarium, built on what was Vanderbilt's tennis courts and opened in 1971. It is regarded as one of the finest planetariums in the country, and was made possible through the William K. Vanderbilt II trust fund. It stands as a symbol not only of Vanderbilt's love of astronomy, but of his philosophy of sharing his interests and knowledge with others.

The magnificently landscaped property is a beautiful sight, with its many reflecting pools, formal gardens, marble statues, fountains, arboretums, the Boxwood Garden, a glass-enclosed arcade and a giant sundial.

William K. Vanderbilt died of a stroke in 1944 at the age of 66. He had donated the estate to Suffolk County, along with a two-million-dollar trust fund for its upkeep. His wife Rosamund remained in the house until her death in 1947. The County then acquired it outright.

The Vanderbilt estate has retained it architectural integrity and setting, and is one of the most distinctive and largely intact examples of its kind built on Long Island's "Gold Coast" during the early twentieth century. As William K. Vanderbilt II wished, his home is now serving as a museum "for the use, education and enjoyment of the public."

THE VELZER HOUSE AND CARETAKER'S COTTAGE

In researching history, one can often find a tremendous amount of information based on the architecture of a particular house or structure. It is important to know what different styles and characteristics mean, and how they relate to our society today and to bygone days. It is in this light that the Velzer House and Caretaker's Cottage in Centerport are very informative. Although there is not much known about the Velzer family except that they were quite wealthy, their home and caretaker's cottage tell their own story — the story of architectural development in our country.

The two buildings are located on adjacent one-acre lots in the unincorporated village of Centerport on Fort Salonga Road (Route 25A). Despite Fort Salonga Road being so well traveled, the homes, now in separate ownership, are surrounded by historic 19th century properties, many of which have been altered. Just east of the two properties is undeveloped land, including wetlands, historically known as Swego. Also referred to as Opcatkontycke, Swego is the Indian place name for the area, and is short for Otswego, meaning "flowing out" or the "wading place creek." When the settlers came, it became known as Cow Harbor Creek.

Situated near picturesque and historically significant areas, the houses, especially the main house called the Velzer Home, are fine examples of the Greek Revival style. It may well be the most distinctive example of vernacular Greek Revival style in the Town of Huntington.

The main house, constructed circa 1830, exhibits Greek Revival style details which have been applied in a conservative manner to a typical three-bay side-entrance settlement period building. The cottage, built much later (circa 1858) is a good example of a 19th century dwelling, containing some Greek Revival details and modeled after the main house.

The Velzer House in Centerport

The Greek Revival style began when archaeological discoveries in the 18th century brought knowledge of Classical Greece to America. A well-known characteristic of the Greek Revival house is that it has the shape of a Classical Greek temple, with the gable-end facade decorated like the Greek Parthenon. The roof, compared to earlier Georgian, Victorian and Gothic Revival styles, has a relatively low slope, with its lower ends usually connecting to form a triangular pediment which is often supported by columns or pilasters. Normally it is trimmed with a bold cornice (the molding located at the junction of the roof and wall surfaces), a frieze (an ornamental band), and an architrave, which is similar to a frieze. In America, however, the Greek Revival style was translated into virtually all shapes. The traditional medieval box shape is among the most common. The most popular color for the Greek Revival interiors and exteriors were various shades of white, with unpainted bricks and stones.

Despite the exterior front facade being strongly symmetrical, the interior of the house was usually not symmetrical at all. The overall look of Greek Revival is simple, clean and uncluttered. It is totally different from the ornately elegant and finely detailed look of a Victorian home. Instead of elegance, the Greek Revival home has a proud and stately appearance.

The Velzer House is a two and one-half story, three-bay clapboard structure flanked by one and one-half story, two-bay wings. The house's central two-story block is oriented with the gable end to the street. The gable has two small six-over-six, double-hung sash windows, and a projecting cornice. The entrance is deeply recessed, and is heavily molded. Six-over-six double-hung sash windows with molded lintels (horizontal pieces over doors or windows) are also featured on all levels.

The gable-roofed side wings are original to the house, and contain many of the same features including clapboard sheathing, projecting cornices and broad friezes. Six-pane fixed attic story windows, and six-over-six, double-hung sash windows with paneled shutters, all with molded lintels, are found on both wings. The west wing has a deeply recessed entrance with a heavily molded surround. A massive exterior end chimney is located at the home's eastern wing.

A one-story clapboard gable-roofed structure was added in the early 20th century, and has a shed-roofed rear extension, which was built on the eastern end of the residence. A modern multi-pane picture window is on the facade.

The caretaker's cottage is located on an adjacent lot, southeast of the main residence. It is a two and one-half story, clapboard structure containing a shallow gable-roofed west wing and a shed-roofed rear extension. The gable end is situated toward the street, and like the main house has a broad projecting cornice. A round-arched, multi-pane window is located at the gable end. Windows are also six-over-six, and are double-hung with sash and flush wooden trim. Tall first floor windows and a side entrance with simple molding distinguishes the main facade. Different from the main house is the gable-roofed porch with tapered columns that shelters the entrance. The three-bay, gable-roofed west wing has a gable dormer and six-over-six double-hung sash windows flanking a modern picture window. Another large picture window was inserted on the east side in the 1980's.

The Caretaker's Cottage

The builder of both homes is unknown, but the use of popular and fashionable architectural styles illustrates the increasing prosperity and economic growth in Huntington during the early 19th century. The Velzer House was one of the earliest residences in Huntington to deviate from the standard, conservative local building traditions of the time, and is also significant in showing the wealth and status of the Velzer family, as the cottage further reflects their continued affluence.

The main house is believed to have been built for an N. Velzer. The Velzer family remained there until about 1909, when ownership was passed to Florence Velzer, who had married J.R. Draper in 1880. Their daughter Edith married James Van Alst, a well-known local architect, and they owned the house from about 1909. The house was commonly known through the 1900's as the Velzer-Van Alst House.

The Velzers owned the cottage until about 1909, but unlike the house it was sold separately to John Bishop, who owned it for many years. A James Van Alst was listed as owner in 1979, when historical site surveys were taken throughout the Town. He is probably a descendant of the Van Alsts who owned the main house.

The Velzer House and Caretaker's Cottage remain residences today, and are listed on the National Register of Historic Places. Both houses have a high degree of architectural integrity, with the Velzer House being the most significant local interpretation of Greek Revival style in the Town of Huntington.

HUNTINGTON STATION

TALES FROM THE VENICE HOTEL

Many years ago Huntington had a number of fine hotels. People would come by horse and carriage, and later by trolley and train, to stay at these establishments. They weren't as large as the hotels we know today, but they did serve their purpose for the traveler. Unfortunately, many of these structures are no longer in existence. There is one surviving building, however, that was a hotel just after the turn of the century. Located in Huntington Station, it was known for many years as the Venice Hotel. Today, local residents know it as Yankee Peddler Antiques.

Situated on New York Avenue, not far from the train station and on the same side, the Venice Hotel was supposedly named after its architect. Huntington Historical Society records indicate the date of initial construction was about 1916, but local people in town argue it was built earlier, possibly in 1906, the year of one of sports history's greatest events, the Vanderbilt Cup auto race. More than 500,000 spectators turned out for the race, which was run on Vanderbilt Motor Parkway from Queens to Lake Ronkonkoma. Hotels, especially near a railroad station, were in demand. Perhaps this was the reason for building the hotel in Huntington Station.

It is believed the Mascaro family built and ran the Venice Hotel, also known sometime later as Mascaro's Bar and Grill. The Mascaros owned the hotel/restaurant/bar until 1979, when it was sold to Mrs. Gloria Smith. She turned the building into an antique center, and sold antiques there for fifteen years. She sold the building and the business to Anne Peace, its current owner, in 1994.

Yankee Peddler Antiques, as it is called, has three floors containing over 10,000 square feet of antiques, with approximately twenty-five dealers selling merchandise. It is Long Island's largest antique emporium. The merchandise consists of 18th, 19th and 20th century formal, country and decorative furnishings, architectural pieces, paintings, pottery, glass, toys, books, and other antiques and memorabilia.

The building is a five-bay, two-story flat roofed structure with an elaborate modillioned cornice. At the top of the building is a stone with the name "Venice" engraved on it. It has twelve-over-one windows, and a one-story enclosed porch across the front. Originally the porch was open, but it was enclosed sometime during the 1930's. The only other exterior change to the building is that the original clapboard was replaced with shingles several years ago. The general layout and structure is virtually original, although some interior partitioning has been added, as well as a basement staircase. The first basement staircase had been located in a storage room on the other side of the building. Next door to the Yankee Peddler is an auto repair shop thought to have been the area where the stable for the guest's horses and carriages was located.

The Venice Hotel, now Yankee Peddler Antiques

Upon entering this unique building, you feel as though you've stepped back in time, and not just because you're surrounded by antiques. Heavy double wood and glass doors lead up a short, wide and very worn wooden staircase. An old fashioned bell rings when the door is opened, announcing guests. With a bit of imagination, it is not difficult to picture the large room above the stairs as a hotel lobby, bar and office. The ornate copper ceiling, which is painted white, stands out immediately and is surrounded by beautiful molding. The room to the right was at one time the dining room; it has the original hardwood floors and dark wainscoting.

The rooms to the left of the main room housed the innkeepers, and a kitchen existed in the rear. The areas to the left and the right of the main room each contain very worn staircases, both of which are made of wood, and lead up to what once was the guest quarters.

Climbing the old dining room staircase, one finds five small rooms on the right, each surrounded with heavy wood molding and glass above the doorway. Although the doors have been removed, you can see where the hinges once hung. Each room has a window decorated with Victorian lace curtains. To the left of the staircase is a larger room that could have been a lobby. There are four rooms in this main area. Above the doorways in large script, either painted on the wood or engraved, are the following: "Parlor," "The Dining Room," "The Boudoir" and "El Toilette." For those paying attention to the many antiques in these rooms, it's easy to miss this interesting bit of history above the doors, but it is well worth the look. Walking across this area, with the floors gently squeaking , you reach the second staircase and another five rooms to the left, similar to those on the right.

The last place to visit in the old hotel is the basement, where refurbishing and repairs are now done on antiques. In this area there is an old brick pizza oven, and even more unusual, painted wall murals. Three murals are located in the area to the left of the staircase, leading down. They are very strange, and are believed to have been painted in the 1930's or 1940's. Two of the murals were discovered behind a leaking, rotted wall, when the wall was removed several years ago. One mural shows a devil walking with a procession of devils, carrying a coffin behind him. A pig with a devil's face and horns also appears. A little further down is a mural of a man hanging by his neck from a tree. Two men nearby are laughing at him. Below the picture the following is faintly written: "The last man who hung up for drinks," and it is signed L. Mascaro. Underneath that is a phrase written in Italian, saying something to the effect that "A man who doesn't pay for his drinks has no honor and will not find happiness." The third mural, which was not hidden away behind a wall, shows a group of men in top hats and long, black coats socializing and drinking. The following is written below: "A gentleman is a gentleman, regardless of color, and always pays for his drinks." It is signed "Uncle Remus."

Two stories concerning the basement may explain the drinking theme of the murals. At one time it was a segregated bar for chauffeurs and hired help, and it may also have been a "speakeasy" during Prohibition—not uncommon in many places in Huntington. When the leaking basement wall was removed, the murals were not the only things found. An old outside entrance and stairway was discovered. Is this where the chauffeurs and help came in and out? Or is it the place where liquor was secretly transported? No one knows for sure, because even today people are reluctant to discuss the goings-on that took place during Prohibition.

As if these murals were not odd enough, it is said that several ghosts haunt the old hotel. I spoke to someone who currently works there (and would like to remain anonymous), as well as a past owner and some older Huntington residents who were familiar with or worked at the hotel, about some of the mysterious stories concerning the building. They each recalled hearing footsteps walking, running or shuffling up and down the two wooden staircases. Many mentioned the strong smell of a woman's unusual perfume in the air, while others have had the strange feeling they were being watched. Owner Anne Peace says that despite the stories, she has yet to experience anything, "although I've never been here late at night," she laughed.

Quite a few of the stories I've written have involved occurrences of "ghostly phenomena." I leave it to the reader to decide whether or not they do in fact exist. I have researched many a place in which ghosts have been seen or heard by the present owners (who, I may add, are all normal, well-respected citizens of Huntington). The people I have interviewed on this matter have never met each other, and yet all have described the same types of ghostly phenomena, time and time again. However, I have toured many a "haunted house" and have yet to experience the unexplained myself.

BIBLIOGRAPHY

Alexander, Irene K., *A History of the Incorporated Village of Lloyd Harbor 1926-1976*, Huntington, New York: West Hills Printing Company, 1976.

American Red Cross, "Clara Baron, Heroic Woman," United States: American Red Cross, 1982.

American Red Cross, "The Red Cross Emblem, Its History, Its Usage, Its Restrictions," United States: American Red Cross, 1980.

Arnason, H.H., *History of Modern Art, Third Edition*, New York: Harry N. Abrams, Incorporated, 1986.

Author unknown, "Dexter K. Cole-Portrait and Biographical Record," source unknown, taken from Northport Historical Society, nd.

Author unknown, "More Long Island History, Miss Oakley's Paper Tells of its Varied Industries for 265 years of Shipbuilding," New York, source unknown, nd.

Author unknown, "Northport at Turn of Century, Described by Louis H. Jones as He Celebrates Golden Anniversary," Huntington, New York: source unknown, nd.

Author unknown, "Red Cross Celebrates 75 Years in Huntington," New York: source unknown, 1992.

Author unknown, "St. John's of Cold Spring Harbor Welcomes New Rector," source unknown, nd.

Author unknown, "The Tree of Sammis," source and date unknown.

Bolton, Charla, "Proposed Old Village Historic District: A Pre-War Suburban Neighborhood," Huntington, New York: Town of Huntington Planning Department, 1987.

Breaux, Adele, *Saint Exupéry in America, 1942-1943, A Memoir*, United States: Associated University Presses, Inc., 1971.

Brush, Russell B., "The Little Cottage," Greenlawn, New York: 1973.

Brush, Russell B., "The Little Cottage," Greenlawn, New York: 1977.

Burr, Jr., Carll S., "The Cradle of the Trotting Horse," New York: *The Rider and Driver*, May 13, 1916.

Cagney, W. Oakley, "Beauty of the Past Thrives Here," New York: *Long Island Press*, 1970.

Cagney, W. Oakley, "Jarvis-Fleet House Saved, Restored," New York: *Long Island Press*, 1971.

Cagney, W. Oakley, "Long Island Long Ago, St. John's Episcopal Church," New York: *Long Island Press*, 1909.

Carr, Edward A.T., *Faded Laurels, The History of Eaton's Neck and Asharoken*, Interlaken, New York: Heart of Lakes Publishing, 1994.

Cold Spring Harbor Whaling Museum, "Report of Curator-1953," Cold Spring Harbor, New York: Whaling Museum, 1953.

Cole Family Bible, "Genealogy of the Cole Family," Northport, New York: 1986.

Corbett, Cynthia Arps, *Useful Art, Long Island Pottery*, Setauket, New York: Society for the Preservation of Long Island Antiquities, 1985.

Credeur, Carol, "The Year They Called Huntington 'Tar Town,' " Huntington, New York: *The Long-Islander*, 1988.

Cronin, David, "The Jarvis-Fleet House," New York: Research Paper, 1966-67.

Dyson, Verne, *Whitmanland*, Brentwood, New York: Verne Dyson Publisher, 1960.

Everett, Helen, "Reclaiming a Long Island Farmhouse," New York: *The American Home Magazine*, 1933.

Friends of Oheka, Inc."Oheka Has a Glorious Past, You can be Part of its Future-Your Questions and Answers About Oheka," Huntington, New York: Friends of Oheka, Inc. Newsletters, 1996.

Godfrey, Shirly, "Huntington Town Views Past and Present," Huntington, New York: *The Long-Islander*, May 30, 1963.

Gould, Zell Morris and Klaber, Henrietta M., *Colonial Huntington, 1653 to 1800*, Huntington, New York, Huntington Press, Inc., 1953.

Greenlawn-Centerport Historical Association, "1991 Fall House Tour," Greenlawn, New York: Greenlawn-Centerport Historical Association, 1991.

Harris, Brad, "Letters From Our Readers," Smithtown, New York: *The Smithtown News*, nd.

Harris, Brad, "News of Long Ago," Smithtown, New York: *The Smithtown News*, nd.

Hendrie, Cynthia and Members of the Northport Historical Society, "A Walking Tour of Bayview Avenue History," Northport, New York: Northport Historical Society, 1973.

Howard, Hugh, *How Old Is This House? A Skeleton Key to Dating and Identifying Three Centuries of American Houses*, New York: The Noonday Press- Farrar, Straus, and Giroux, 1989.

Howard, Hugh, *How Old Is This House?*, New York: The Noonday Press, Farrar, Straus & Giroux, 1989.

Huntington Fire Department, "Fire Department of Huntington Village," Huntington, New York: Huntington Fire Department, 1959.

Huntington Historical Society, "Old Town Hall District," Huntington, New York: Huntington Historical Society, nd.

Huntington Historical Society, "Huntington Multiple Resource Area, Old Town Green Historic District," Huntington, New York: Huntington Historical Society, nd.

Huntington Historical Society, "Tour of Ferguson Castle," Huntington, New York: Huntington Historical Society, 1966.

Kilpatrick, Bette and Lott, Roy E., "Knowing Huntington- Wide, Long Swing Winds Up Tour of the Township", Huntington, New York: *The Long-Islander*, nd.

King, Robert B., *Ferguson's Castle, A Dream Remembered*, Hicksville, New York: Exposition Press, 1978.

King, Robert, B., *Raising a Fallen Treasure: The Otto H. Kahn Home, Huntington, Long Island*, Mattituck, New York: The Mad Printers of Mattituck,1985.

Langhans, Rufus B., "Huntington Historic Houses," The Delamater-Bevin Mansion, New York: *Northport Journal*, nd.

Langhans, Rufus B., "Huntington Historic Houses-The John Green House," Huntington, New York: Huntington Historic Preservation Commission, 1986.

Langhans, Rufus B., "Huntington Historic Markers," Huntington, New York: Town of Huntington, 1992.

Langhans, Rufus B., "Letter to the Town Board, re: Whitman-Rome House," Huntington, New York: 1969.

Langhans, Rufus B., *Huntington National Register of Historic Places*, Huntington, New York: Town Historian's Office, 1994.

Langhans, Rufus B., "Huntington Historic Houses- The Velzer House and Caretaker's Cottage," New York: *Architectural Heritage Year*, 1986.

Langhans, Rufus, B., *Huntington Historic Cemeteries*, Huntington, New York: 1990.

Long Island Independent, "Build All Distinctive Crafts At Knutson Central Shipyard," New York, *Long Island Independent*, 1938.

Lott, Roy E., "Historic Huntington," Huntington, New York: *The Observer*, 1968.

Lott, Roy E., "Keeping Time for the Town," Huntington, New York: *The Long-Islander*, 1965.

Ludwig, Alfred W., "From Masheen to 1,250 G.P.M., A History of the Protection Engine Company #1 of the Huntington Fire Department 1843 to 1876," Huntington New York: Department Historian, 1978.

Ludwig, Alfred W., "History of the Huntington Fire Department 1858 to 1966," Huntington, New York: Department Historian, 1966.

MacLachlan, C.H., "Movies, Actors, and Memories," Huntington, New York: *The Long-Islander*, 1979.

Metcalf Jr., Reginald H., "The Jarvis Fleet House- Historical Sketch," Huntington, New York: Reginald Metcalf, 1974.

Northport Historical Society Press Release, "Northport Historical Society Displays Unique Doll House as a Celebration of New York, 1986," New York: Northport Historical Society, 1986.

Northport Historical Society, "The John C. Smith, House, Circa 1860," Northport, New York: Northport Historical Society Tour, 1970.

Northport Journal, "Historic View of Northport Business," New York: *Northport Journal*, nd.

O'Brien, Tim, "Northport's Proud Heritage," New York: *Long Island Heritage*, 1982.

Obituary, "Louis H. Jones," Huntington, New York: source unknown, 1965.

"Old Town Green Historic District," New York: Huntington Multiple Resource Area, Suffolk County, nd.

Partride, William Ordway, *Nathan Hale, The Hale Patriot*, New York and London: Funk and Wagnalls Company, 1902.

Platt, Hon. Henry C., "Old Times in Huntington. An Historical Address," Huntington, New York: *Long Islander Print*, 1876.

Price, Kirk, " 'Tar Town' Huntington's Secret Disgrace", New York: *Newsday*, nd.

Raciopio, Patricia, "The Seymour Boat Shop," Northport, New York: source unknown, nd.

Randall, Monica, *The Mansions of Long Island's Gold Coast*, New York: Hasting House Publishers, 1979.

Ritch, Carol Lee, "Huntington to Sell Antique Town Hall," Northport, New York: *The Observer*, 1980.

Rode, Suzanne M. Townsend, "The Little Cottage," Greenlawn, New York: 1954.

Rosen, Lucille, *Commack-A Look Into the Past*, Commack, New York: Commack Board of Education, School District Print Shop, 1970.

Sammis, Romanah, *Huntington-Babylon Town History*, Huntington, New York: Huntington Historical Society, 1937.

Singer, Anita, "Commack Methodist Church Celebrates 190th Year", Huntington, New York: *The Long-Islander*, September 13, 1973.

Smith, Mark, "Huntington Pottery: The Brown Brother Years", New York: Mark Smith, nd.

St. John's Church, *The Parish Register, Part II- Special 150th Anniversary Edition, St. John's Church, 1985-86,*" Cold Spring Harbor, New York: St. John's Church, 1986.

Sunday Digest, "Huntington Town Hall Seeing Its Final Months," New York: *Sunday Digest,* 1978..

"The Ancestors of Greenlawn and Centerport," Hartford Branch of the Burr Family, United States: nd.

The Huntington Historical Society, *Images of Huntington II*, New York: Printed by Natwest Bank NA, 1973.

The Kelsey Outrage, Philadelphia: E.E. Barclay and Co., 1873.

The Long-Islander, "Town Landmark Up For Auction," Huntington, New York: *The Long-Islander,* 1980.

The Long-Islander, "Abrams' Shipyards Under Management of Thomas Knutson," Huntington, New York: *The Long-Islander,* 1938.

The Long-Islander, "March is Red Cross Month," Huntington, New York: *The Long-Islander,* 1980.

The Long-Islander, Historical Society Will Make Pilgrimage to the 'Town Spotte,'" Huntington, New York: *The Long-Islander,* 1941.

The Northport Chamber of Commerce, "Northport, Long Island, A Place for All Seasons," New York, The Northport Chamber of Commerce, nd.

The Northport Historical Society Museum, "Northport's Great Shipbuilding Era," Northport, New York: Northport Historical Society Museum, nd.

The Northport Historical Society, "A Walking Tour of Northport's Historic Main Street," Northport, New York: *The Observer,* nd.

The Observer, "A Walking Tour of Northport's Historic Main Street", Northport, New York: The Northport Historical Society, nd.

The Observer, "Cottage Has Rich History," Northport, New York: *The Observer,* 1986.

The Observer, "Students, Scouts, Kiwanis, Clean Up Historical Plot", Northport, New York: *The Observer,* November 6, 1973.

The Observer, "Speakeasy in Northport? We Found it!", Northport, New York: *The Observer,* 1982.

The Salem Herald, "Quest to Preserve Castle," Salem, West Virginia: *The Salem Herald,* 1968.

"This Old Cemetary Has Its Own Battle History," New York: Newspaper unknown, , nd.

Todd, Charles Burr, *A General History of the Burr Family,* New York: The Knickerbocker Press, 1902.

Toedtman, Jim, "Mysteries of a Grand Old Castle Kindles Spirits of Adventurers," New York: *Newsday,* 1970.

Town Historian's Office, "John Green House, 167 East Shore Road, Huntington," Suffolk County, New York: Multiple Resource Area, nd.

Vagts, Christopher R., *Huntington in Our Time,* Huntington Station, New York: Huntington Historical Society, Hamilton Lithographers, Inc., 1975.

Weber, Harvey A., *Centerport,* Centerport, New York: H.B. Davis Co., 1990.

Zsedely, Dr., "An Interview with Louis H. Jones," Northport, New York: The Northport Library, c.1962.

INDEX